CUISINART™
FOOD PROCESSOR COOKING

CUISINART™
FOOD PROCESSOR COOKING

CARMEL BERMAN REINGOLD

A DELTA SPECIAL

A DELTA SPECIAL

Published by
Dell Publishing Co., Inc.
1 Dag Hammarskjold Plaza
New York, New York 10017

CUISINART is the trademark of Cuisinarts, Inc.
of Stamford, Connecticut.

DELTA ® TM 755118, Dell Publishing Co., Inc.

ISBN: 0-440-51604-8

Printed in the United States of America

Sixth Delta Printing—March 1978

Contents

INTRODUCTION:
THE CAREFREE WORLD OF
THE FOOD PROCESSOR

If you love to cook but lack the time to prepare gourmet meals, or if you would like to do more entertaining but are bored with the idea of kneading another pie crust dough, you should explore the world of food processor cooking. Thanks to a variety of food processors, you can prepare gourmet meals and enjoy fresh foods without spending long hours in the kitchen.

Each food processor is really many machines in one. Some of them combine the handy features of an electric blender, meat grinder, grater, slicer, and dough maker. Others have accessories that whip, mix, blend, and knead dough. Still others function as juicers, can openers, pasta makers, potato peelers, and ice cream freezers. Almost all of the machines will perform such specific tasks as the following:

Grate bread crumbs and cheese
Grind raw meat for Steak Tartare, hamburgers, meat loaf, pâté, and sausage

Chop vegetables for stews, soups, and casseroles
Shred cabbage for slaw
Shred potatoes for pancakes
Puree potatoes for creamy mashed potatoes
Knead a pie crust in thirty seconds
Puree fruit for jam
Grind fresh horseradish
Slice potatoes for home fries
Grind peanuts into delectable peanut butter.

One of the first food processors to gain popular acceptance in the United States was the Cuisinart™. Such authorities on food and cooking as Craig Claiborne, Julia Child, and James Beard have helped to introduce the food processor into American kitchens. Claiborne has called the Cuisinart unit the "20th-century French Revolution . . . the equivalent of an electric blender, electric mixer, meat grinder, food sieve, potato ricer and chef's knife rolled into one."

The Cuisinart machine is actually a scaled-down version of a much larger food processor, the Robot Coupe, which has been used in the kitchens of French restaurants for years. As the food processor gained popularity, other European and American manufacturers began to produce smaller models for home use. Many American-made machines have been around for a long time, but it has taken the surge of interest in the Cuisinart unit to alert consumers to the usefulness of food processors. The range of choice is quite large, and as the average selling price is over two hundred dollars, it is important to find the food processor that is right for your cooking needs and your kitchen. Before you buy, take a look at the buyer's guide section of this book.

BUYER'S GUIDE TO FOOD PROCESSORS

There are perhaps a dozen food processors on the market that perform a variety of functions. Some of these machines have many attachments, others only a few; some take up a lot of space in your kitchen, while others are quite compact. With all this variety, there is one food processor that is just right for you. In order to decide which processor that is, you should compare the machines to see which one offers you the most of what you want and need. You should also consider what equipment you already have and the functions it performs. If you have a high-powered blender, you won't need a processor with a blender attachment. If you have a dough maker, you needn't look for a machine with a dough hook. If your kitchen is already equipped with a machine that whips cream and egg whites, then you won't need a processor that whips.

This chapter tells you what you need to know about the nine leading food processors. Here is information about the basic equipment, functions, and capabilities of the Cuisinart™, Bosch Magic Mixer™, Braun®, KitchenAid®, NuTone, Oster® Kitchen Center™, Starmix, Sunbeam Mixmaster, and Vita Mix 3600® food processors. Whichever you choose, you can be assured of gaining an extra pair of hands in the kitchen.

Cuisinart™ Food Processor

BASIC EQUIPMENT:

Motor base
Cylindrical clear 7-cup plastic bowl and cover
Pusher that fits into the feed tube of the cover
1 stainless steel knife blade
1 plastic mixing blade
1 stainless steel slicing disc
1 stainless steel shredding disc
1 plastic spatula

OPTIONAL ATTACHMENTS:

Thin slicing disc
Fine grating disc
French fry cutter

FUNCTIONS:

The Cuisinart processor chops, slices, shreds, grinds, kneads, blends, purees, and grates.

It will chop vegetables, grate cheese, chop meat, crush ice, make nut butters, grind nuts, make pastry dough, make bread and cracker crumbs, and mash potatoes. It will also slice and shred vegetables, grind fish, prepare pasta doughs, puree soups, puree fruit for jam, and prepare sauces such as mayonnaise and Hollandaise.

The Cuisinart unit can knead only one loaf of bread dough at a time. Heavy mixtures must be prepared in two or more steps. While it will whip cream and beat egg whites, it does not perform in this capacity as a conventional cream- or eggbeater. The mixture will become thick enough to use, but it will not increase greatly in volume because air has not been beaten into it.

The Cuisinart unit is compact, takes up little space, and is easily assembled for use. One of the beauties of this machine is that with very few attachments—only four blades, in fact—it performs as many functions as the more complicated appliances with many more attachments. A Cuisinart machine on a countertop takes up about twice the space of a blender, and the blades can be stored in a bowl beneath the counter. Since the Cuisinart processor is so easy to clean, there's no hesitation in using it to chop a single onion or slice a couple of carrots.

Bosch Magic Mixer™

BASIC EQUIPMENT:

Motor base

Two attachment centers: one for mixing, beating, and vertical cutting; another for liquefying and blending. The attachments for these two centers are:

5½-quart plastic mixing bowl and cover
Kneading arm (dough hook)
Dual stainless steel whisks (beaters)
1½-quart blender
Stainless steel slicing and shredding equipment with 2 slicing and 2 shredding blades

OPTIONAL ATTACHMENTS:

Centrifugal juice extractor for fruits and vegetables
Meat grinder, with the following accessories:

Fruit press for preparing fruit for jam
Grating attachment
Biscuit piping attachment (cookie press)
Pasta maker
Sausage shaper
Coffee mill, which also grinds nuts and herbs
Ice cream maker
Lemon squeezer
Grain mill
Extrusion shredder with set of discs for making cole slaw and slicing vegetables in large quantity
Potato peeler

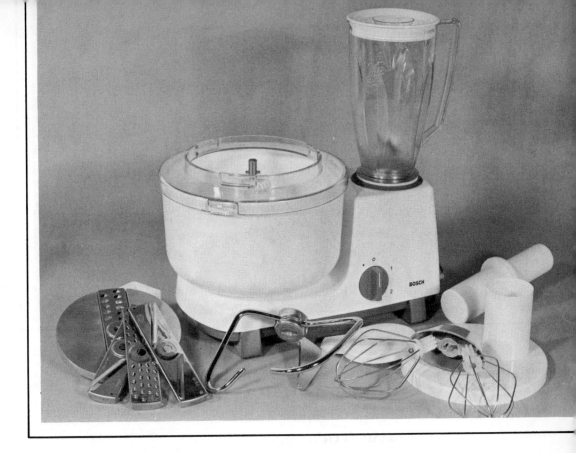

FUNCTIONS:

The Bosch unit beats, mixes, whips, kneads, blends, slices, shreds, liquefies, and purees. With the optional attachments it can also grate, grind meat, prepare juice, press cookies, make pasta, stuff sausages, grind coffee, make ice cream, peel potatoes, and prepare tomatoes or fruits for canning.

The Bosch will slice, shred, or grate potatoes or other vegetables; extract juice from fruit or vegetables; knead dough for bread; whip batters for cakes; blend soups, drinks, or sauces; make spaghetti noodles; and puree fruits for jam.

With all of its optional attachments, the Bosch can do just about everything. The only drawback is that all of those parts will require storage space in your kitchen.

Braun® Kitchen Machine

BASIC EQUIPMENT:

Motor base
4½- and 1½-quart plastic mixing bowls
32-ounce blender
Whisk
Dough hook
Shredder-slicer with five stainless steel cutting blades

OPTIONAL ATTACHMENTS:

Meat grinder
Citrus juicer
Coffee grinder, which also grinds nuts and cheese

FUNCTIONS:

The Braun unit mixes, beats, whips, shreds, grates, blends, and kneads dough. With the optional attachments it can also grind meat, prepare juice, and grind coffee, nuts, and cheese.

The Braun will whip both cream and egg whites; slice, grate, and shred vegetables and potatoes in a variety of ways; knead all kinds of pastry doughs as well as bread doughs; prepare icings and cream fillings; make pasta dough; blend sauces; and puree vegetables and fruits. With the optional attachments it will also grind meat, grind coffee, nuts, and cheese, and prepare citrus juice.

The Braun is a good-looking combination of mixer, blender, and cutter, and its attachments don't require too much storage space.

The KitchenAid K-45

KitchenAid® K-45 and K5-A

BASIC EQUIPMENT:

The K-45 has a motor stand, 4½-quart stainless steel bowl. The K5-A has a 5-quart stainless steel bowl. Both machines come with:

Wire whip for whipping cream and egg whites
Dough hook
Flat beater for general mixing

OPTIONAL ATTACHMENTS FOR BOTH THE K-45 AND K5-A:

Meat, nut, and vegetable grinder
Sausage stuffer
Grain mill
Can opener

The KitchenAid K5-A

Vegetable slicers and shredders, both rotary and vertical
Citrus juice maker
Ice cream maker
Silver buffer

FUNCTIONS:

Both KitchenAid® machines beat, mix, whip, and knead. With
the optional attachments, they can also grind meat; grate, slice,
and shred vegetables; make ice cream; stuff sausages; prepare
citrus juices; and open cans.

People who bake are especially fond of the KitchenAid® They
feel that it is one of the best machines available for kneading
all kinds of dough. The KitchenAid® also does a splendid job
on whipping cream and egg whites for soufflés. It does not have
a blender attachment, but with its other optional attachments
you can grind meat for your own pâtés and sausages, make
cole slaw, and prepare a bountiful four quarts of ice cream.

NuTone Appliance Food Center

BASIC EQUIPMENT:

> Motor base built into the kitchen counter
> 4-quart plastic bowl and mixer
> 48-ounce blender
> Knife sharpener

OPTIONAL ATTACHMENTS:

Power post to be used with:
> Meat grinder
> Shredder slicer
> Can opener

Also available:
> Ice crusher
> Citrus fruit juicer

FUNCTIONS:

The NuTone basic unit is a combination mixer and blender. However, with the optional attachments it grinds meats; shreds, grates, and slices vegetables; crushes ice; and makes fruit juice.

The NuTone will whip cream and egg whites. It will also whip potatoes and cake frostings. It will blend sauces and drinks, puree soups, grind meat into a perfect Steak Tartare, and shred or grate vegetables from a small flake to a proper slice.

The NuTone does not have a dough hook for kneading heavier bread doughs, but the mixer can do lighter cookie or batter doughs.

The great advantage to the NuTone is that the motor is built right into the kitchen counter. The motor is hidden beneath the counter, and all that is visible on top is a flush-mounted counterplate that occupies only a few inches of space. The attachments can be stored beneath the counter and removed one at a time as you need them. Your counter is available to you the rest of the time, and because each piece of equipment attaches directly to the counterplate, you never see a trailing electric cord.

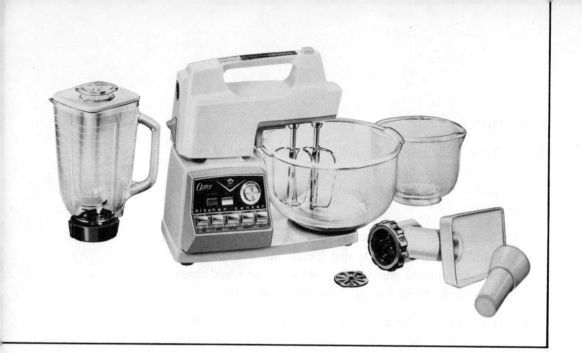

Oster® Kitchen Center™

BASIC EQUIPMENT:

Motor base
1½ - and 4-quart stainless steel or glass bowls
5-cup blender
Mixer arm with two beaters
Food grinder with fine and coarse cutting discs

OPTIONAL ATTACHMENTS:

Dough hook
Ice crusher
Salad maker for slicing vegetables, fruits, potatoes
Foodcrafter slicer/shredder for slicing, shredding, and
    grating with 3 cutting blades

FUNCTIONS:

The Oster® Kitchen Center™ is a combination mixer, blender, and grinder. With the optional attachments it will also knead dough; crush ice; and shred, slice, and grate vegetables in a variety of ways.

Oster has long been famous for its blender, and the blender in the Kitchen Center has 10 speeds. The mixer does a fine job on egg whites and cream, and will cream butter and sugar, mash potatoes, and whip up light omelets. The grinder prepares meat for hamburgers, chops leftover meat for hash and croquettes, and grinds fish for appetizers. The optional attachments do make it a complete "kitchen center" as its name states.

Starmix

BASIC EQUIPMENT:

Motor base
5-quart stainless steel bowl with feed-tube lid and plastic
   cover
1½-quart blender
Dough hook
Beater
5 cutting blades for grating, shredding, fine shredding,
   thick slicing, and thin slicing
Spatula

OPTIONAL ATTACHMENTS:

Citrus press
French fry cutter
Ice cream maker
Juice extractor
Meat grinder

FUNCTIONS:

The Starmix mixes, blends, stirs, kneads, chops, shreds, beats, whips, slices, and grates. With the optional attachments it will also grind meat, make citrus and vegetable juices, and prepare ice cream and French fries.

The Starmix is a compact machine. The dough hook, beater, and cutting blades all operate in connection with the 5-quart stainless steel bowl, and the blender and other attachments can be stored until needed. The mixing bowl is large enough so that you can work with quantities of potatoes, dough, and vegetables when mashing, kneading, or slicing. The dough hook allows the machine to knead heavy bread dough, and the variety of cutting blades means that chocolate or cheese can be finely grated, while vegetables can go from a fine shred to a thin or thick slice. The meat grinder is a valuable optional attachment to purchase along with the basic unit.

Sunbeam Mixmaster Mixer

BASIC EQUIPMENT:

Motor base
Pair of dough hooks
Two bowls, 4-quart and 1½-quart, either stainless steel
or heat-resistant clear glass
Pair of beaters

OPTIONAL ATTACHMENTS:

Juicer
Meat grinder/food chopper with an extra power unit that
can be attached to the basic machine

FUNCTIONS:

The Sunbean Mixmaster will knead dough, beat, whip, mix, and with the optional attachments prepare citrus juice and chop meat and vegetables.

This is the right machine for the person who wants an inexpensive appliance that specializes in mixing, beating, whipping, and kneading. The machine can prepare one loaf of bread dough at a time, as well as knead dough for biscuits, muffins, and tea rings. It can also be used for cakes, frostings, salad dressings, mashed potatoes, and custards. There's a 12-speed dial attached to the mixer that indicates the proper speed for everything from folding in dry ingredients to whipping cream and preparing icing. The optional juicer and meat grinder/food chopper adds an extra dimension to this compact unit, and the beaters can be removed from the motor stand to be used as a portable hand beater, to be taken directly to a double boiler or saucepan, if needed.

Vita Mix 3600®

BASIC EQUIPMENT:

Motor base
72-ounce stainless steel container with pressurized spigot
See-through plastic lid with clamps and funnel top
Wooden tamper

OPTIONAL ATTACHMENTS:

None

FUNCTIONS:

The Vita Mix 3600® mixes, grinds grain, and kneads dough. It makes whole fruit and vegetable juices, blends, makes nut butters, cooks soups and sauces, prepares ice cream, crushes ice, grinds meat, purees, and chops. It does not slice or whip.

This is a most unusual food processor. It is completely self-contained, and needs no extra attachment. It is something of a superblender, and it works on the principle of blade reversal. The motor is extremely powerful, and when the blades are moving in a forward direction they go at 265 miles an hour; when reversed with a flick of the switch, they move at 530 miles an hour. With such speed, the machine can actually grind grain into flour, and then mix the flour with other ingredients to turn out a bread dough in four minutes.

In addition to kneading dough, the Vita Mix also grinds meat for Steak Tartare and hamburgers; it will even produce ice cream in a few seconds. Before you serve the ice cream, you can dazzle your family or friends by preparing hot vegetable soup in the Vita Mix. The soup won't be cooked, as the Vita

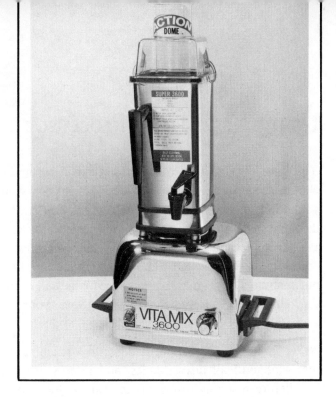

Mix has no heating unit; but the vegetable juices and the water will be hot, thanks to the action of the powerful motor and the friction of the blades.

The Vita Mix also makes "total juice," using whole fruits and vegetables, and it will chop vegetables and grate potatoes if they are first cut into 1- to 2-inch chunks.

Because this machine is so different from any other appliance on the market in that it is operated by a speed control knob and an impact lever, it may take a little experimentation before you are able to process foods with ease. Once you learn how to achieve the desired textures for foods, the Vita Mix will produce perfect peanut butter, grated carrots, chopped eggs and cabbage, and ground meat.

You should note that the Vita Mix 3600® has a three-pronged plug that requires a compatible outlet or an adaptor. Check your kitchen to see if it has the proper wiring and fuses for this heavy-duty machine.

Using Your Food Processor

You have decided to acquire a food processor and you have chosen the one that seems absolutely right for your cuisine, your kitchen, and your life-style. Before you start using the machine, read all the directions and literature provided by the manufacturer and then read it all again. None of these machines is so complicated that you won't be able to master it, but manufacturers give explicit directions and cautions, and they should be followed if you want to use your machine to best advantage.

Never insert your fingers or hands into a machine that's moving; wait until all discs, blades, and motors have come to a halt before reaching inside to see that the food you are processing is of the desired texture. Handle all knife blades, grinders, and discs with care, and keep them out of the reach of children. Many of these tools are quite sharp-edged.

Don't expect your machine to do more that it can do. If you are working with large quantities of food and your machine has a small capacity, process the food in two or more batches. These food processors work so quickly that even if you have to process in two steps, it still won't take more than a very few minutes.

Once you have started using your machine, you'll find that you can easily adapt many of your favorite recipes for preparation in the food processor. Go forward fearlessly, knowing that the processor will give you all the help you need to become a fine, creative cook.

APPETIZERS

For many people, the appetizer is the most exciting part of any meal, because it offers a variety of interesting foods that are piquant and stimulating to the palate. And appetizers provide a great opportunity to experiment with new foods and ideas from other countries. A new foreign dish is often better introduced as an appetizer than as a main course.

It's easy to substitute appetizers for a first course and serve them away from the dining table. Let guests help themselves to exotic dips, vegetable spreads, and finger foods while you serve the drinks, the wine, or chilled goblets of tomato juice garnished with long celery swizzle sticks. If you are serving a dinner of many courses, prepare one or two of your favorite appetizers, just enough to make your guests eager for the next course.

Céleri Rave Rémoulade

1 pound celery root, peeled and cut into 2-inch pieces
1 teaspoon salt
2 teaspoons lemon juice
3 tablespoons Dijon mustard
3 tablespoons boiling water
½ cup olive oil
1 tablespoon wine vinegar
Salt and freshly ground black pepper to taste

Shred celery root in food processor. Remove to a bowl and sprinkle with salt and lemon juice. Allow celery root to marinate for 30 minutes, then rinse in cold water, drain, and dry on paper towels.

Now blend mustard and boiling water in food processor. Add oil in a slow, steady stream and continue blending until sauce is thick. Add vinegar gradually and continue blending. Add salt and pepper.

Spoon sauce from food processor into a bowl and stir in celery root. Allow vegetable to marinate for at least 2 hours before serving.

Serves: 6 to 8

Cuisinart processor: Shredding disc for processing celery root; plastic mixing blade for blending sauce ingredients

Other processors: Attachments manufacturer recommends for shredding and blending

Eggplant Caviar

It may be Eggplant Caviar in English, but to the Rumanians, who insist they invented this dish, it's called Putla Jel. *By either name, it's an unusual appetizer that goes especially well with Mideastern pita bread and your favorite cocktail.*

1 large eggplant
1 medium onion, cut in half
1 small green pepper, seeded and sliced
Juice of ½ lemon
½ cup olive oil (or more, to taste)
Salt and freshly ground black pepper to taste
¼ teaspoon sharp red pepper flakes (optional)

Place eggplant in broiler, and broil until skin is charred and eggplant is soft to the touch. Turn eggplant every 10 minutes or so. Eggplant will be cooked in 20 to 30 minutes, depending on size of vegetable and your broiler.

When eggplant is cooked, remove from broiler and allow to cool. Peel and cut eggplant into large pieces. Place eggplant pieces and all other ingredients except pepper flakes in food processor and process until mixture is a coarse puree.

Spoon puree into a bowl, and chill. Sprinkle red pepper flakes on top before serving.

Serves: 4 to 6

Cuisinart processor: Steel knife blade

Other processors: Blender or attachments manufacturer recommends for grinding and mixing

Eggplant Puree

This delightful appetizer is served at the Intercontinental Hotel in Old Jerusalem.

1 large eggplant
1 clove garlic
⅓ cup tahini (sesame seed paste)
Juice of 1 lemon
⅓ teaspoon ground cumin
Salt to taste
Freshly ground black pepper to taste
1 tablespoon olive oil

Broil eggplant, turning from side to side, until skin is charred and eggplant is soft to the touch. Depending on the size of your eggplant and broiler, this should take from 20 to 30 minutes.

Remove eggplant from the broiler, allow to cool, and then peel. Cut eggplant into chunks, place in food processor, and puree. Add other ingredients and blend thoroughly. Correct seasoning and serve as a dip with large, flat Mideastern bread or sesame seed crackers.

Serves: 4 to 6

Cuisinart processor: Steel knife blade

Other processors: Blender or attachments manufacturer recommends for chopping and mixing

Hummus Bi Tahini

"What is it? How do you make it?" Be prepared for questions when you serve this interesting mixture of chick-peas and sesame seed paste. The ingredients may not seem so fascinating by themselves, but in combination they create a culinary delight. The origin of this dish is Mideastern; and if you want to sound truly knowledgeable, hummus *is the word for chick-peas and "tahini" signifies the rich sesame seed paste.*

1 cup cooked chick-peas
1 tablespoon olive oil
Juice of 2 lemons
3 cloves garlic
Salt to taste
½ cup tahini (sesame seed paste)
¼ teaspoon strong paprika

Place chick-peas, olive oil, lemon juice, and garlic in food processor. Puree. Add salt, tahini, and paprika and blend until mixture is a creamy paste. If mixture is too thick, you may add more lemon juice. Correct seasoning and pile *hummus bi tahini* into a glass bowl. Garnish with ripe black olives and tiny cherry tomatoes. Serve with pita bread or thin crackers.

Serves: 4 to 6

Cuisinart processor: Steel knife blade

Other processors: Attachments manufacturer recommends for grinding and mixing

Shrimp Toast

6 canned water chestnuts
⅓-inch piece fresh ginger
½ pound shrimp, shelled and deveined
1 scallion, cut into 3 pieces
1 egg yolk
1½ teaspoons cornstarch
1 tablespoon sherry wine
Salt to taste
Freshly ground black pepper to taste
2 egg whites
2 cups vegetable oil
3 slices slightly stale white bread, crusts trimmed, cut into quarters

Place water chestnuts and ginger in food processor and chop fine. Add shrimp, scallion, and egg yolk and blend. Add cornstarch and sherry and continue processing until mixture is a paste. Add seasonings. Remove mixture from processor to a large bowl. Wash and dry processor bowl thoroughly.

Place egg whites in processor and beat until thick. Fold beaten egg whites into shrimp mixture, using a spatula or a large wooden spoon. Do not use processor.

Heat vegetable oil in a wok or large skillet. Spread bread quarters with shrimp mixture and slip bread into hot oil, shrimp side down. Brown, and turn and brown other side. Remove from pan, drain, and serve at once.

Serves: 4 to 5

Cuisinart processor: Steel knife blade for preparation of shrimp mixture; plastic blade for egg whites

Other processors: Attachments manufacturer recommends for chopping, and for beating egg whites

Mr. T. T. Wang owns and is the chef at Shun Lee Palace, one of the best Chinese restaurants in New York. Mr. Wang, who was introduced to us by one of his captains, Eddie Liu, has generously shared two of his very special appetizer recipes.

T. T. Wang's Chinese Shrimp Strawberries

1 cup hulled sesame seeds
1 tablespoon red food coloring (optional)
½ pound shrimp, shelled and deveined
2 canned water chestnuts
1 egg white
½ teaspoon salt
1 grind of fresh white pepper
1 tablespoon sherry wine
1 tablespoon cornstarch
1 teaspoon sesame oil
12 two-inch long strips of green pepper, sliced thin
4 cups salad oil

Mix sesame seeds with food coloring and spread seeds on an ovenproof dish. Place dish in a 200-degree oven for 5 to 7 minutes. Stir seeds once or twice and remove dish from oven when seeds are dry.

Place shrimp, water chestnuts, egg white, salt, pepper, sherry, cornstarch, and sesame oil in food processor and blend. Turn the machine on and off, scraping mixture down from sides of the bowl, and blend until mixture is a thick paste.

Spoon mixture into a bowl and refrigerate for ½ hour.

To Form Strawberries: Take 1 tablespoon of shrimp mixture, form into a ball shape, and roll in colored sesame seeds until shrimp ball is well coated with seeds. Form each shrimp ball into a strawberry shape and decorate with a green pepper strip for the stem. Refrigerate Shrimp Strawberries for an hour or so, until they are firm.

Heat salad oil in a deep fryer, wok, or large skillet until oil is sizzling hot. Fry strawberries approximately 3 to 5 minutes on each side, until they are crisp. Drain and serve at once. You'll have about 12 strawberries, and depending on your other hors d'oeuvres, this will:

Serve: 3 to 4

Cuisinart processor: Steel knife blade

Other processors: Attachments manufacturer recommends for grinding and mixing

T. T. Wang's Green Pepper Puffs

3 small green peppers
2 canned whole water chestnuts
¼ pound lean pork, trimmed and cut into cubes
1 scallion, cut into 3 pieces
1 egg white
1 teaspoon sherry wine
½ teaspoon salt
1 grind white pepper
½ teaspoon sesame oil
½ tablespoon cornstarch
1 egg white
½ cup flour
¼ cup water
1 teaspoon salad oil
1 teaspoon baking powder
4 cups salad oil

Cut peppers into wide strips. Three peppers should yield 12 pieces. Discard seeds and membrane. Place water chestnuts, pork cubes, scallion pieces, and egg white in food processor. Process until smooth, and then add sherry, salt, pepper, sesame oil, and cornstarch and process into a smooth paste. Spread mixture on green pepper strips, smoothing with the back of a spoon or fingers.

Place egg white, flour, water, 1 teaspoon of salad oil, and baking powder in processor and blend thoroughly. Coat each slice of stuffed pepper with this batter.

Heat salad oil in a deep fryer, wok, or large skillet until oil is sizzling. Reduce heat and cook puffs in oil, about 5 minutes on each side, until they are golden brown. (Don't cook for less than 10 minutes all told, or pork may not be done.)

Drain and serve at once.

Serves: 3 to 4

Cuisinart processor: Steel knife blade

Other processors: Attachments manufacturer recommends for grinding and mixing

Gail's Deviled Eggs

1 dozen hard-cooked eggs, peeled and cut lengthwise
½ cup homemade mayonnaise
½ small onion
1 teaspoon lemon juice
1 teaspoon Dijon mustard
¼ teaspoon salt
¼ teaspoon pepper
2 sprigs parsley
Sweet paprika

Remove yolks from whites. Reserve whites. Place all ingredients except egg whites and paprika in food processor and blend until smooth, about 20 seconds. With a spoon or pastry tube, fill egg whites with yolk mixture. Sprinkle eggs with paprika.

Serves: 8 to 10

Cuisinart processor: Steel knife blade

Other processors: Blender or attachments manufacturer recommends for chopping and mixing

Ham Devilish Eggs

8 hard-cooked eggs
½ cup mayonnaise
2–3 small sweet pickles, cut in half
1 teaspoon Dijon mustard
Salt and freshly ground white pepper to taste
1 or 2 slices of boiled ham, cut into 4 or 5 pieces
¼ teaspoon mild paprika

Peel eggs, cut in half lengthwise, and spoon yolks into food processor. Add all other ingredients and process until mixture is thoroughly smooth. Fill egg-white halves with mixture and garnish with a small sliver of pickle, if you wish.

Serves: 6 to 8

Cuisinart processor: Steel knife blade

Other processors: Blender or attachments manufacturer recommends for chopping and mixing

Lenke's Hungarian Egg Salad

American egg salad always seemed bland to my mother, who makes her egg salad with onions, rendered chicken fat, and plenty of black pepper. This piquant version takes egg salad out of the ordinary category.

8 hard-cooked eggs
1 large onion, cut into quarters
½ cup rendered chicken fat
Salt and freshly ground black pepper to taste

Peel eggs, cut in half, and place in food processor. Add all other ingredients and process until mixture is thoroughly blended. You may add more chicken fat if you wish. Correct seasoning and serve a large dollop of egg salad on an individual lettuce leaf. Makes a very fine first course or can be used as a sandwich spread.

Serves: 4 to 5

Cuisinart processor: Steel knife blade

Other processors: Attachments manufacturer recommends for chopping and mixing

Hungarian *Lecso* and Smoked Sausage

Hungary, a small and not terribly rich country, is the source of many fine recipes that make a little meat go a long way. But no Hungarian worthy of the name would touch a money-saving recipe that was flat or uninteresting. Here's a spicy appetizer that's inexpensive but rich in flavor.

½ cup olive oil
2 medium onions
2 large green bell peppers
1 pound very ripe red tomatoes
2 teaspoons sugar
¼ teaspoon salt
½ tablespoon sweet paprika
½ teaspoon hot paprika, or to taste
½ pound Hungarian cooked and smoked Kolbasz sausage,
   or your favorite smoked sausage

Heat olive oil in a large skillet, and while oil is heating, chop onions and green peppers coarsely in food processor. Add onions and peppers to oil in skillet and cook gently for 10 to 15 minutes. Meanwhile, puree the tomatoes coarsely in the food processor and add to skillet. Cook, stirring, for an additional 10 to 15 minutes. Add seasonings and correct to taste. Slice sausage in food processor and add to mixture in skillet, stirring until sausage is thoroughly hot. Serve with hand-cut chunks of caraway-seeded rye bread and dry red wine.

Serves: 4 to 6

Cuisinart processor: Steel knife blade

Other processors: Attachments manufacturer recommends for slicing and pureeing

---

Taramasalata

This fish roe appetizer has long been a favorite of guests at Greek and Mideastern restaurants. Tarama is the salted and dried pressed roe of the gray mullet, and is found canned in many small Greek food shops and gourmet stores. If you can't find tarama, you can use smoked cod's roe, available in stores that sell smoked fish. If you use smoked cod's roe, remember to remove the outer membrane before proceeding with the recipe.

> **3 slices thick-cut white bread**
> **1 cup milk**
> **3 ounces tarama**
> **1 clove garlic**
> **Salt and white pepper to taste**
> **1 slice of onion**
> **Juice of 1 lemon**
> **6 tablespoons olive oil**

Cut crusts from bread, and soak slices in milk. Place tarama in food processor. Chop thoroughly. Squeeze milk from bread and add bread, garlic, seasoning, and onion to processor. Blend thoroughly, adding lemon juice gradually. Correct seasoning and continue blending until mixture is a light and creamy pink paste. Serve with Mideastern pita bread and tiny Greek black olives.

Serves: 4

Cuisinart processor: Steel knife blade

Other processors: Blender or attachments manufacturer recommends for grinding and mixing

Avocado Tuna Spread

2 medium ripe avocados
1 seven-ounce can tuna, drained
½ cup mayonnaise, or more, to taste
Dash of Tabasco
Salt to taste
Freshly ground black pepper to taste

Peel avocado, and cut flesh into large pieces. Place pieces in food processor and add tuna, mayonnaise, and Tabasco. Puree and blend thoroughly. Season to taste. Serve with buttered rounds of sourdough bread or rolls.

Serves: 6 to 8

Cuisinart processor: Steel knife blade

Other processors: Attachments manufacturer recommends for chopping and mixing

Frilly Dip

½ head iceberg lettuce
4 tablespoons olive oil
2 tablespoons wine vinegar
2 scallions
¼ teaspoon salt
Freshly ground black pepper to taste
¼ teaspoon thyme
¼ teaspoon sage
1 eight-ounce package cream cheese, cut into 4 pieces

Place ¼ head of iceberg lettuce in food processor. Add all other ingredients, except cream cheese and remaining ¼ head of lettuce. Process until lettuce is coarsely chopped and blended with other ingredients. Add cream cheese and the rest of the lettuce and process until ingredients are blended. Correct seasoning. Serve with crackers or toasted pumpernickel fingers.

Serves: 4 to 6

Cuisinart processor: Steel knife blade

Other processors: Attachments manufacturer recommends for chopping and mixing

Dutch Cheese Balls

3-inch round Edam cheese, with a red wax coat
¼ pound sweet butter, cut into 6 or 7 pieces
½ teaspoon sharp mustard
1 tablespoon brandy
Dash of Tabasco
¼ teaspoon mild paprika

Slice off top of cheese, and with a knife or melon ball cutter, scoop out as much of cheese as possible, leaving outside shell intact. Place cheese and other ingredients in food processor and blend thoroughly. Pile mixture back into hollowed cheese shell and garnish with a few more shakes of paprika.

Serves: 6 to 10, approximately

Cuisinart processor: Steel knife blade

Other processors: Blender or attachments manufacturer recommends for shredding and mixing

Camembert Cashew Appetizer

12–15 cashew nuts
¼ pound sweet butter
¼ pound Camembert cheese, room temperature
¼ cup sweet white wine

Toast cashews in a 300-degree oven until nuts are lightly browned. Be careful not to burn them. Place nuts in food processor and grind until fine. Cut butter into 6 or 7 pieces and add to nuts in processor. Gently remove rind from Camembert, and after cutting cheese into approximately 6 or 7 pieces, place in processor. Add wine and process, turning machine on and off so that mixture is well blended but does not reach melting stage. Heap in a bowl and chill. Serve with crackers and a bowl of celery and carrot sticks.

Serves: About 6

Cuisinart processor: Steel knife blade

Other processors: Blender or attachments manufacturer recommends for grinding and mixing

Biscuits of Brie

4 ounces ripe Brie cheese
2 ounces sweet butter, room temperature
1 egg
¼ teaspoon salt
2 or 3 grinds of white pepper
Pinch of cayenne pepper
1 cup flour

Gently remove crust from Brie. Cut cheese into chunks and place in food processor. Cut butter into two pieces and add to processor. Add egg and seasoning and blend. Gradually add flour. Turn machine on and off, scraping dough down from sides, and process until dough is thoroughly blended. If dough seems too soft, add another tablespoon of flour. Remove dough from processor, wrap in wax paper, and chill until firm.

Roll biscuit dough out until it is about ¼ inch thick, and cut into 1-inch rounds. Heat oven to 350 degrees and bake for 15 to 20 minutes or until biscuits are lightly browned.

Serves: 4 to 6

Cuisinart processor: Steel knife blade

Other processors: Attachment manufacturer recommends for kneading dough. If processor has a dough hook, you may double this recipe.

Pineapple Walnut Spread

1 eight-ounce package cream cheese, cut into 6 pieces
½ cup shelled walnuts
3 slices canned pineapple
1 tablespoon pineapple syrup
⅛ teaspoon cinnamon

Place all ingredients in food processor. Chop and blend until smooth. Serve with date-nut bread or thin toast fingers.

Serves: 4 to 6

Cuisinart processor: Steel knife blade

Other processors: Blender or attachments manufacturer recommends for chopping and mixing

Irene's Caraway Cheese Spread

1 three-ounce package cream cheese, cut into 3 pieces
¼ pound sweet butter, cut into 5–6 pieces
1 small onion, cut into quarters
½ teaspoon mild paprika
¼ teaspoon caraway seeds

Place all ingredients in food processor. Blend thoroughly. Pile into a dish or bowl and garnish with a sprinkling of paprika on top. Serve with crackers and slices of cucumber.

Serves: 6 to 8

Cuisinart processor: Steel knife blade

Other processors: Attachments manufacturer recommends for chopping and mixing

Spring Salad Dip

1 stalk celery, cut into 3 pieces
1 carrot, cut into 3 pieces
¼ green pepper, cut into chunks
2 radishes
3 slices sweet cucumber pickle
3 sprigs parsley
1 teaspoon dried chives
1 pimiento
½ teaspoon salt
¼ teaspoon freshly ground black pepper
1 eight-ounce package cream cheese, cut into chunks

Place all ingredients except cream cheese in food processor. Chop for about 10 seconds. Add cream cheese and process until smooth. Use as a dip with fresh raw vegetables or crackers.

Serves: 4 to 5

Cuisinart processor: Steel knife blade

Other processors: Blender or attachments manufacturer recommends for chopping and mixing

Flavored Butters

In France, butter comes in many more flavors than just salt or sweet. These beurres composés *are available in endless variety and are created by combining butter with herbs, spices, raw vegetables, and fish. These seasoned butters can be used to flavor other dishes or they can be used as dips and as spreads. Keep a small pot of* beurre composé *in your refrigerator to create an instant hors d'oeuvre for unexpected company or to use as a topping for vegetables.*

Anchovy Butter

1 two-ounce can anchovies, drained
1 scallion, cut into 2 or 3 pieces
¼ pound sweet butter, cut into 4–6 pieces

Place anchovies and scallion pieces in food processor and chop for about 20 seconds. Add butter and continue processing until well blended.

Yield: Approximately ½ cup

Cuisinart processor: Steel knife blade

Other processors: Blender or attachments manufacturer recommends for chopping and mixing

Herb Butter

¼ cup mixed fresh dill, parsley, and chives
¼ pound sweet butter, cut into 4–6 pieces

Place herbs in food processor and chop for about 20 seconds. Add butter and continue processing until smooth.

Yield: ½ cup

Cuisinart processor: Steel knife blade

Other processors: Blender or attachments manufacturer recommends for chopping and mixing

Lemon Parsley Butter

¼ cup fresh Italian parsley
1 tablespoon lemon juice
¼ pound sweet butter, cut into 4–6 pieces
1 tablespoon heavy sweet cream
3 grinds of white pepper

Place parsley in food processor and chop for approximately 20 seconds. Add remaining ingredients and process until smooth.

Yield: ½ cup

Cuisinart processor: Steel knife blade

Other processors: Blender or attachments manufacturer recommends for chopping and mixing

Nutty Butter

1 cup mixed nuts
¼ pound sweet butter, cut into 4–6 pieces
Salt to taste

Place nuts in food processor and process until chopped. Add butter and salt and blend 2 to 3 minutes until smooth.

Yield: 1 cup

Cuisinart processor: Steel knife blade

Other processors: Blender or attachments manufacturer recommends for grinding and mixing

Tuna Butter

¼ pound sweet butter, cut into 4–6 pieces
½ cup drained tuna fish
1 hard-boiled egg, cut in half
½ small onion
1 teaspoon lemon juice
Salt and freshly ground black pepper to taste

Place all ingredients in food processor and blend until mixture is thoroughly smooth.

Yield: 1 cup

Cuisinart processor: Steel knife blade

Other processors: Blender or attachments manufacturer recommends for chopping and mixing

SOUPS

"Beautiful Soup, so rich and green,
Waiting in a hot tureen!
Who for such dainties would not stoop?
Soup of the evening, beautiful Soup!
Soup of the evening, beautiful Soup!"

> as sung by the Mock Turtle,
> in *Alice in Wonderland*

Soup, whether rich and green in a hot tureen or creamy white and chilled in your best cut-glass bowl, can be beautiful. There's something soothing about soup, something that speaks of meals prepared as they were long ago, with care and a genuine interest in pleasing.

Beautiful soup can be still more beautiful, thanks to the food processor. Vegetables can be chopped more easily for a thick minestrone, beans can be turned into a rich puree for a truly velvety Mexican bean soup, and potatoes and onions made to melt into the cream of a fine vichyssoise. Whether you serve it as a beginning course or as a meal in itself, soup is easier to prepare with your food processor.

Chicken Curry Soup

1 carrot, cut into 3 or 4 pieces
2 onions, cut into quarters
2 stalks celery, each cut into 3 or 4 pieces
½ cup sweet butter
2 tablespoons flour
1 tablespoon curry powder
1 large apple, peeled, cored, and quartered
2 cups cooked chicken, cut into cubes
8 cups chicken broth, canned or homemade
Salt to taste
Freshly ground white pepper to taste
1 cup heavy sweet cream

Place carrot, onions, and celery in food processor and chop. Heat butter in a large skillet and sauté vegetables until they're translucent. Add flour and curry powder and cook, stirring for 2 to 3 minutes. Place apple and chicken in food processor and grind until fine. Add cooked vegetables to processor and gradually add 2 cups of chicken broth, blending thoroughly as you go. You may have to do this in two or more steps. When mixture is thoroughly blended, pour into a large saucepan and stir in remainder of chicken broth. Add seasonings. Bring to a simmer and cook for 10 minutes. Remove from heat and stir in cream.

Serves: 8 to 10

Cuisinart processor: Steel knife blade

Other processors: Blender or attachments manufacturer recommends for chopping, grinding, and pureeing

Creamy Avocado Soup

1 large ripe avocado, or 2 small ones
1 scallion, cut into 3 pieces
3 cups chicken broth, homemade or canned
1 cup heavy sweet cream
Salt to taste
Freshly ground black pepper to taste
2 tablespoons freshly minced dill

Peel avocado, cut into chunks, and place in food processor. Add scallion and puree thoroughly. Gradually add chicken broth and blend. You may have to do this in two steps. Remove soup from processor and stir in cream. Season to taste. Chill. Garnish with minced dill when serving.

Serves: 6

Cuisinart processor: Steel knife blade

Other processors: Blender or attachments manufacturer recommends for pureeing and mixing

DANISH CUCUMBER SOUP
Courtesy College Inn Broth

Danish Cucumber Soup

5 medium cucumbers
½ medium onion, cut into 2 pieces
2 tablespoons sweet butter
¼ cup flour
2 quarts chicken broth, canned or homemade
2 bay leaves
Salt to taste
Freshly ground white pepper to taste
1 cup light sweet cream
1 tablespoon lemon juice
8 sprigs fresh dill

Peel cucumbers. Chop one cucumber in food processor and set aside. Slice remaining 4 cucumbers in food processor and set aside. Chop onion in food processor. Heat butter in a large saucepan and sauté chopped onion for 3 minutes. Blend in flour and cook 2 to 3 minutes more, stirring constantly. Add chicken broth gradually, stirring. Add all but 8 cucumber slices to soup mixture and stir in bay leaves, salt, and pepper. Cover, and simmer for 10 minutes. Remove bay leaf and puree soup in food processor. You may have to do this in two or more steps. When soup is thoroughly pureed, stir in cream, lemon juice, and chopped cucumber. Heat slowly. Serve with a slice of cucumber atop each bowl and sprinkle with dill.

Serves: 8

Cuisinart processor: Steel knife blade and slicing disc

Other processors: Blender or attachments manufacturer recommends for chopping, slicing, pureeing, and mixing

Fish Soup Bonne Auberge

One summer in the south of France I had a dreadful cold, and reluctantly went off to the Bonne Auberge Restaurant knowing that I wouldn't be able to eat a thing. The waitress looked at me sympathetically, and before I could explain that I wouldn't be eating dinner, she placed a large soup tureen in front of me, handed my husband the menu, and indicated that the soup was all for me. Only good manners made me taste it. It was hot and delicious, retaining the essence of the flavor of fish without being the least bit fishy. I ate every drop and felt completely revived.

The Mediterranean fish generally used in this recipe are not available in this country, but the soup can be made with other fish as long as they are fresh.

1 large onion, cut into quarters
4 cloves garlic, cut into halves
2 green peppers, seeded and cut into 4 slices each
1 carrot, cut into 3 or 4 pieces
1 stalk celery, cut into 4 pieces
¼ cup olive oil
5 ripe tomatoes, peeled and cut in half
3 pounds fillets of assorted fish: cod, halibut, haddock, bass
½ teaspoon Herbes de Provence or
   ¼ teaspoon thyme, 1 crushed bay leaf, ¼ teaspoon fennel
¼ teaspoon dried orange peel
1 cup dry white wine or dry vermouth
3 quarts water
Salt and freshly ground black pepper to taste
French bread rounds, toasted, and rubbed with a cut garlic
   clove

Chop onion, garlic, green peppers, carrot, and celery in food processor. Heat oil in large soup pot and add chopped vegetables. Cook over low heat until vegetables are tender, but do not let them brown. Chop tomatoes in food processor and add to pot. Cook, stirring constantly, for another 5 to 10 minutes.

Cut the fish fillets into cubes and add to vegetable mixture. Continue cooking for an additional 5 minutes and keep stirring. Stir in herbs and orange peel and add wine, water, salt, and pepper. Cover, bring to a simmer, and cook for 30 to 40 minutes.

Puree soup thoroughly in a food processor. You may have to do this in two or more steps. Return to soup pot and heat through. Correct seasoning and serve with a toasted French bread round in each bowl.

Serves: 8 to 10

Cuisinart processor: Steel knife blade

Other processors: Attachments manufacturer recommends for chopping and pureeing

Chinese Good Fortune Fish Soup

¾ pound fillet of sea bass or striped bass
2 egg whites
⅓ cup water
1 teaspoon salt
½ teaspoon sugar
1 tablespoon cornstarch
1 tablespoon peanut oil
5 cups chicken broth
2 scallions, chopped
¼ cup canned bean sprouts
6 sliced canned water chestnuts

Make sure fish fillet is completely free of bones. Cut the fillet into chunks and put in food processor. Add egg whites, water, salt, sugar, cornstarch, and oil and process until mixture is thoroughly blended into a paste.

Fill a large pot with two quarts of water. Form paste into 1-inch fish balls and drop into water. Bring water to a simmer and then remove fish balls to a large strainer or colander. Rinse fish balls with cold water.

Pour chicken broth into a large saucepan and add drained fish balls. Slowly bring broth to a simmer, and simmer for 8 to 10 minutes. Add scallions, bean sprouts, and water chestnuts to broth; correct seasoning and serve.

Serves: 6

Cuisinart processor: Steel knife blade

Other processors: Attachments manufacturer recommends for grinding and mixing

Vichyssoise

2 leeks, white ends only, cut into pieces
1 medium onion, cut into quarters
3 tablespoons sweet butter
4 medium potatoes, peeled
4 cups chicken broth, homemade or canned
2 cups light sweet cream
Salt to taste
Freshly ground white pepper to taste
3 teaspoons chopped chives or scallion tops

Chop leeks and onion in food processor. Melt butter in two-quart pot and sauté leeks and onion over low heat until translucent. Slice potatoes in food processor and add to sautéed vegetables. Add chicken broth to pot. Cover and cook until potatoes are tender. Puree soup in food processor (you may have to do this in two steps), until thoroughly blended. Pour soup into a large bowl, stir in cream and seasonings, and chill. Serve in individual soup cups with chopped chives or scallions as a garnish.

Serves: 6 to 8

Cuisinart processor: Steel knife blade and slicing disc

Other processors: Blender or attachments manufacturer recommends for chopping, slicing, and mixing

Chilled Pear Soup

4 fresh pears, peeled, cored, and quartered
1 small apple, peeled, cored, and quartered
2 tablespoons lemon juice
1 potato, peeled and quartered
1 celery stalk, cut into 4 pieces
1 scallion, cut into 3 pieces
Salt to taste
¼ teaspoon curry powder
2 cups chicken broth, homemade or canned
2 cups light sweet cream
Dash of cinnamon

Place pears, apple, lemon juice, potato, celery, and scallion in food processor and chop. Remove mixture to a large saucepan and add salt, curry powder, and chicken broth. Bring to a simmer and cook uncovered for 10 minutes. Return soup to food processor and blend until completely smooth. You may have to do this in two steps. Stir in cream and chill thoroughly. Serve garnished with a dash of cinnamon.

Serves: 6

Cuisinart processor: Steel knife blade

Other processors: Blender or attachments manufacturer recommends for pureeing and mixing

CHILLED PEAR SOUP
Courtesy California Tree Fruit Agreement

Mexican Black Bean Soup

In Mexico, dinner is not considered a proper meal unless soup is served. And dinner, which starts between one and two o'clock in the afternoon, continues for well over two hours through course after delicious course of appetizers, soup, fish, salad, roast, and dessert. After a large bowl of soup, the tendency for this North American is to stop eating, but one mustn't insult the host and hostess. Promising to diet tomorrow, we eat on and look forward to a post-lunch siesta.

1 pound black beans
6 cups water
1 pound lean pork, trimmed and cubed
1 tablespoon oil
2 onions, cut into quarters
2 cloves garlic
2 tomatoes, peeled and halved
1 green pepper, seeded and cut into 4 pieces
¼ teaspoon ground cumin
¼ teaspoon thyme
⅛ teaspoon chili pepper
Salt to taste
Freshly ground black pepper to taste
Fresh lime slices

Presoak beans if necessary, or follow directions on package. Place beans in a large kettle with water and bring slowly to a boil. Fry pork cubes in oil until brown and add to bean pot.

Place onions, garlic, tomatoes, and green pepper in food processor and puree thoroughly. Add vegetable mixture and seasonings to bean pot and cook approximately 4 hours or until beans are tender.

Puree bean soup in food processor. You may have to do this in two or three steps. Correct seasoning. Heat soup until it is piping hot and serve with lime slices.

Serves: 6 to 8

Cuisinart processor: Steel knife blade

Other processors: Blender or attachments manufacturer recommends for pureeing and mixing

♪♪*♪*

Harry's Perfect Gazpacho

There are many recipes for this cold Spanish soup, but this is my husband's very own version. It is the result of his search for the perfect gazpacho, and many of our friends think he has found it.

3 cloves garlic
1 medium onion, quartered
1 cucumber, peeled and cut into 4 pieces
3 ripe tomatoes, peeled and cut into halves
1 green pepper, seeded and cut into 4 pieces
Salt to taste
Dash of cayenne pepper
¼ cup wine vinegar
¼ cup olive oil
¾ cup tomato juice
Ground cumin to taste
Freshly ground black pepper to taste

GARNISH:

1 cup croutons
3 tablespoons olive oil
1 garlic clove, cut in half
1 cucumber
1 onion
1 green pepper

Place garlic, onion, cucumber, tomatoes, and green pepper in food processor and puree. Add remaining ingredients and blend mixture completely. You may have to do this in two steps. Pour soup into a bowl or your favorite marmite and chill.

Before serving, sauté croutons in olive oil in which you are also sautéeing garlic halves. Coarsely chop cucumber, onion, and green pepper in food processor and pass in separate bowls when serving the soup.

Serves: 8 to 10

Cuisinart processor: Steel knife blade

Other processors: Blender or attachments manufacturer recommends for pureeing and chopping

✻ༀ✻ༀ✻

Hearty Lentil 'n' Sausage Soup

2 carrots, each cut into 3 or 4 pieces
2 stalks celery, each cut into 3 or 4 pieces
2 medium onions, cut into quarters
6 or 7 sprigs Italian parsley
4 tablespoons vegetable oil or rendered bacon drippings
2 tablespoons flour
6 cups hot chicken or beef broth, homemade or canned
¼ teaspoon thyme
1½ cups washed lentils
Salt to taste
Freshly ground black pepper to taste
½ pound of cooked Polish Kielbasa sausage, cut into
   ½-inch rounds

Place carrots, celery, onions, and parsley in food processor and chop. Heat oil or bacon drippings in a 5-quart pot and sauté vegetables until they're translucent and barely tender. Stir in flour and cook for 2 to 3 minutes over low heat, stirring constantly. Slowly pour in hot chicken or beef broth, stirring steadily so that flour and broth are well blended. Bring mixture to a simmer and add all remaining ingredients except sausage. Cover pot and cook approximately two hours or until lentils are completely cooked.

Pour soup into food processor and puree. You may have to do this in two or more steps. Pour soup back into pot, add sausage, and heat thoroughly. Serve with pumpernickel or black bread.

Serves: 6 to 8

Cuisinart processor: Steel knife blade

Other processors: Blender or attachments manufacturer recommends for chopping and pureeing

Aunt Vicenza's Minestrone

¼ pound salt pork, cut into 3 pieces
1 clove garlic
1 small onion, cut in half
5 sprigs Italian parsley
2 stalks celery, each cut into 3 pieces
2 carrots, each cut into 3 pieces
¼ cup olive oil
2 tablespoons tomato paste
2 potatoes, each cut in half
2 zucchini, each peeled
1 cup cooked chick-peas
6 cups chicken or beef broth, homemade or canned
Salt and freshly ground black pepper to taste
1 cup small shell pasta
Freshly grated Parmesan cheese

Place salt pork, garlic, onion, parsley, celery, and carrots in food processor. Chop. Place olive oil in a large soup pot, heat gently, and add all vegetables from food processor. Cook until slightly brown. Stir in tomato paste and add ½ cup of broth to dilute. Cook 5 minutes. Slice or chop potatoes and zucchini and add to soup pot. And chick-peas, remainder of broth, and salt and pepper. Cook 30 to 40 minutes, until vegetables are completely tender. Add pasta and cook until shells are firmly cooked, or *al dente*, approximately 8 to 10 minutes. Correct seasoning. Serve with grated cheese.

Serves: 6 to 8

Cuisinart processor: Steel knife blade and slicing disc

Other processors: Attachments manufacturer recommends for chopping or slicing

SAUCES
AND
SALAD DRESSINGS

A sauce or flavorful salad dressing goes a long way in telling family and friends that you have made something special just for them. And while bottled sauces and dressings are readily available, they have none of the extra flavor that is offered by a brown sauce or a garlic mayonnaise made in your own kitchen.

In the past, preparing a homemade sauce took time, too much time for anyone involved in events outside of the kitchen. Now the food processor has taken the drudgery out of making your own sauces. The processor will chop onions, garlic cloves, and tomatoes in seconds and blend them into homemade mayonnaises to create a variety of flavored salad dressings. Not too long ago, a French garlicky *rouille* sauce or an Italian *pesto* called for pounding in a mortar with a pestle. Today, the food processor makes quick work of these and many other sauces.

The recipes that follow will guide you in adapting your own favorite sauce and dressing recipes for preparation in the food processor.

Mayonnaise

Homemade mayonnaise should be prepared in small batches, since, unlike the store-bought variety, it contains no preservatives. You should plan to use it within five days.

I

1 egg
1 teaspoon dry mustard
1 tablespoon wine vinegar
½ teaspoon salt
¼ teaspoon lemon pepper
1 cup vegetable oil

Place all ingredients, except oil, in food processor. Blend for about 10 seconds. Add oil slowly to processor in a steady stream. Mixture will begin to thicken. Process the mixture longer for thicker mayonnaise.

Yield: 1 cup

Cuisinart processor: Plastic blade

Other processors: Blender or attachment manufacturer recommends for beating

II

2 egg yolks
¼ teaspoon salt
2 teaspoons Dijon mustard
3 teaspoons lemon juice
1 cup olive oil

Place all ingredients except oil in food processor and blend for about 10 seconds. Add oil slowly to the processor in a steady stream. Mixture will begin to thicken. Because this recipe calls for 2 egg yolks, you may find that this mayonnaise thickens more quickly than that in the preceding recipe.

Yield: 1½ cups

Cuisinart processor: Plastic blade

Other processors: Blender or attachment manufacturer recommends for beating

III

2 egg yolks
1 egg
½ teaspoon Dijon mustard
¼ teaspoon salt
2 teaspoons lemon juice
1 cup olive oil
1 cup salad oil
Freshly ground white pepper to taste

Place egg yolks, egg, mustard, and salt in food processor. Process for about 10 seconds. Add lemon juice and add oil slowly in a steady stream. Check flavor of mayonnaise after adding half the oil and correct seasoning. Continue processing until mixture thickens.

Yield: 2½ cups

Cuisinart processor: Plastic blade

Other processors: Blender or attachment manufacturer recommends for beating

Aioli

Aioli is a staple in most French kitchens, but it comes as a happy surprise to most Americans who have never thought of combining mayonnaise and garlic. The French use aioli in a variety of ways, from adding it to fish soups to make them more garlicky, to spreading it on cold meats that are frequently served for Sunday suppers. Aioli is a useful mayonnaise to keep in the refrigerator; a few dabs can bring leftovers to life again.

4 cloves garlic
1 egg
1 teaspoon dry mustard
1 tablespoon wine vinegar
½ teaspoon salt
¼ teaspoon lemon pepper
1 cup vegetable oil

Place garlic in food processor and chop fine. Remove garlic and set aside. Place remaining ingredients, except oil, in food processor and blend for about 10 seconds. Add oil slowly to processor in a steady stream until mixture begins to thicken. Add the garlic to the processor and continue processing for another 20 seconds.

Yield: About 1 cup

Cuisinart processor: Steel knife blade for chopping garlic; plastic blade for mayonnaise

Other processors: Blender or attachments manufacturer recommends for fine chopping and beating

Herb Mayonnaise for Fish

½ cup Italian parsley or basil or ½ cup combination of both
1 egg
1 teaspoon dry mustard
1 tablespoon wine vinegar
½ teaspoon salt
¼ teaspoon lemon pepper
1 cup vegetable oil

Chop parsley or basil in food processor and remove and set aside. Place remaining ingredients, except oil, in food processor and blend for about 10 seconds. Add oil slowly to processor in a steady stream until mixture begins to thicken. Add the chopped greens to the processor and continue processing for another 20 seconds.

Yield: About 1 cup

Cuisinart processor: Steel blade for chopping greens; plastic blade for mayonnaise

Other processors: Blender or attachments manufacturer recommends for chopping and beating

Tartar Sauce

1 egg
1 teaspoon dry mustard
1 tablespoon wine vinegar
½ teaspoon salt
¼ teaspoon lemon pepper
1 cup vegetable oil
2 sprigs parsley
1 tablespoon capers
1 tiny sweet gherkin pickle, chopped

Place the first 5 ingredients in food processor and blend for about 10 seconds. Add oil slowly to processor in a steady stream until mixture begins to thicken. Add the parsley, capers, and chopped pickle to the processor and continue processing for another 20 seconds.

Yield: About 1 cup

Cuisinart processor: Plastic blade

Other processors: Blender or attachment manufacturer recommends for beating

Sauce Rémoulade

1 clove garlic
2 rolled fillets of anchovies with capers
4 sprigs herbs (may be just parsley, or parsley and chives, or parsley and fresh tarragon)
1 hard-boiled egg, cut in half
1 teaspoon Dijon mustard
2 cups homemade mayonnaise

Place garlic, fillets of anchovies with capers, herbs, egg, and mustard in food processor and chop and blend thoroughly. Stir mixture into mayonnaise.

Yield: Approximately 2½ cups

Cuisinart processor: Steel knife blade

Other processors: Blender or attachments manufacturer recommends for chopping and mixing

Sweet Walnut Sauce for Egg Noodles

1 cup shelled walnuts
4 tablespoons sugar, or more, to taste
2 cups sour cream

Place nuts in food processor and chop coarsely. Add sugar and sour cream and blend mixture thoroughly. Add more sugar, to taste. Serve Walnut Sauce over cooked egg noodles either as a dessert or a luncheon dish. Before topping with Walnut Sauce, you may drizzle noodles with melted butter for extra richness.

Yield: Sauce for 4 or 5 servings of egg noodles

Cuisinart processor: Steel knife blade

Other processors: Attachments manufacturer recommends for grinding and mixing

Green Goddess Salad Dressing

6 fillets of anchovies
3 scallions, each cut into 3 pieces
6 sprigs Italian parsley
8 blades fresh chives
½ teaspoon dried tarragon
2 cups homemade mayonnaise
2 tablespoons tarragon vinegar

Place anchovies, scallions, parsley, and chives in food processor and chop finely. Add mayonnaise and blend. Stir in vinegar.

Yield: Approximately 2½ cups

Cuisinart processor: Steel knife blade

Other processors: Blender or attachments manufacturer recommends for chopping and mixing

Russian Dressing

1 egg
1 teaspoon dry mustard
1 tablespoon wine vinegar
½ teaspoon salt
¼ teaspoon lemon pepper
1 cup vegetable oil
2 tablespoons ketchup
2 tablespoons relish

Place first 5 ingredients in food processor and blend for about 10 seconds. Add oil slowly to processor in a steady stream until mixture begins to thicken. Add the ketchup and relish to the processor and continue processing for another 20 seconds.

Yield: About 1 cup

Cuisinart processor: Plastic blade

Other processors: Blender or attachment manufacturer recommends for beating

Roquefort French Dressing

¾ cup olive oil
½ teaspoon salt
¼ teaspoon mild paprika
Freshly ground black pepper to taste
¼ cup wine vinegar
3 ounces or 4 tablespoons Roquefort cheese

Place oil, salt, paprika, pepper, and vinegar in food processor and blend thoroughly. Add Roquefort cheese and continue processing until mixture is thoroughly blended.

Yield: Approximately 1 cup

Cuisinart processor: Steel knife blade or plastic blade

Other processors: Blender or attachment manufacturer recommends for mixing

Basic Brown Sauce

Mix brown sauce with the pan juices of roast beef or roast pork to make a rich gravy. Combine it with sautéed mushrooms to enliven filet slices or mix with a quarter cup of white wine to serve over roasted veal or chicken. Brown sauce will keep for several weeks in your refrigerator if tightly sealed, or it may be frozen for future use.

1 carrot, cut into 3 or 4 pieces
1 small onion, cut in half
1 stalk celery, cut into 3 or 4 pieces
¼ pound sweet butter
4 tablespoons flour
1 tablespoon tomato paste
4 parsley sprigs
½ bay leaf
¼ teaspoon thyme
6 cups beef broth, homemade or canned

Place carrot, onion, and celery pieces in food processor and chop. Heat half the butter in a large skillet, add chopped vegetables, and sauté until tender. Meanwhile, melt remainder of butter in a large saucepan over low heat, stir in flour, and cook until flour is a tan color. When flour is tan, remove from heat. Stir in tomato paste and add chopped vegetables and the butter they have sautéed in. Add herbs and broth and stir thoroughly to prevent flour from lumping. Place over low heat, bring to a simmer, and cook for 1 hour. Skim off any fat or scum that rises to the surface as the sauce cooks. If sauce is too thick, you can add more beef broth or ½ cup dry vermouth. If sauce is too thin, increase heat and cook until sauce is reduced.

Pour sauce into food processor and blend thoroughly. You may have to do this in two or more steps. Return sauce to saucepan. Bring to simmer one more time and remove from heat. Serve immediately or refrigerate for future use.

Yield: About 3 cups

Cuisinart processor: Steel knife blade

Other processors: Blender or attachments manufacturer recommends for chopping and mixing

Hollandaise

¼ pound sweet butter, melted
3 egg yolks
2 tablespoons lemon juice
¼ teaspoon salt
⅛ teaspoon fresh white pepper

Place melted butter and all other ingredients in food processor. Process until sauce is thick, approximately 2 to 3 minutes. (If you're using the Cuisinart, don't lose patience. Hollandaise made in this food processor takes a little longer to thicken than it would in a blender.)

Yield: About 1 cup

Cuisinart processor: Plastic blade

Other processors: Blender or attachments manufacturer recommends for beating

Fresh Horseradish Cream Sauce

**1 two-inch piece of fresh horseradish root, scraped and cut
into 2 pieces**
1 cup sour cream
Sugar to taste
Salt and freshly ground black pepper to taste

Finely grate horseradish in food processor. Add other ingredients and blend thoroughly. Bring to a simmer in a small pot; correct seasoning. Serve with hot boiled beef or smoked fish.

Yield: About 1½ cups

Cuisinart processor: Steel knife blade

Other processors: Attachments manufacturer recommends for fine grating and mixing

Mornay Sauce

4 ounces Swiss cheese, cut into cubes
¼ pound sweet butter, cut into 6 pieces
¼ cup flour
2 cups milk
1 teaspoon salt
2 sprigs parsley

Place all ingredients in food processor and process until mixture is thoroughly smooth. Pour sauce into a small saucepan and cook over low heat until mixture comes to a boil and begins to thicken. Stir occasionally.

Yield: 2 cups

Cuisinart processor: Steel knife blade

Other processors: Blender or attachment manufacturer recommends for mixing

Rouille

In France, rouille *is the traditional sauce served with bouillabaisse. It can also be served with a fish stew, and if you're a real* rouille *lover you might enjoy it as piquant sauce for baked fish fillets.*

3 canned red pimientos
¼ teaspoon Tabasco
1 medium boiled potato
3 cloves garlic
4 or 5 fresh basil leaves, or 1 teaspoon dry basil
½ cup olive oil
Salt and freshly ground black pepper to taste

Place all ingredients, except oil, in food processor. Puree thoroughly. Change blades and add olive oil in a slow but steady stream; process until thick and blended. Correct seasoning. If sauce is too thick, blend in 2 or 3 tablespoons hot water.

Yield: About 1 cup

Cuisinart processor: Steel knife blade for preliminary ingredients; plastic blade for blending olive oil

Other processors: Blender or attachments manufacturer recommends for pureeing and mixing

Tomato Sauce

1 six-ounce can tomato paste
2 cups canned whole stewed tomatoes
1 stalk celery, cut into 3 pieces
1 clove garlic
1 small onion cut in half
Sugar to taste
Salt to taste
¼ teaspoon hot red pepper flakes (optional)

Place all ingredients in food processor and blend thoroughly. Correct seasoning and pour sauce into a heavy saucepan. Cook over low heat for 30 minutes. This is delicious over meat loaf, chicken, or baked fish fillets.

Yield: About 2½ cups

Cuisinart processor: Steel knife blade

Other processors: Blender or attachments manufacturer recommends for chopping and mixing

Italian Tomato Sauce

1 medium onion
2 cloves garlic
3 sprigs Italian parsley
1 tablespoon oil
1 twenty-eight-ounce can whole tomatoes in thick tomato
   puree
1 six-ounce can tomato paste
3 fresh basil leaves (or 1 teaspoon dried basil flakes)
1 tablespoon sugar
1 teaspoon salt
¼ teaspoon pepper
2 cups water

Place first 3 ingredients in food processor and chop finely. Heat oil in a large saucepan and sauté onion mixture until lightly browned.

Process next 6 ingredients in food processor until smooth. You may have to do this in two or more steps, adding tomato mixture to saucepan as you process. After entire tomato mixture is in saucepan, stir in water. Simmer sauce over low heat for about 2 hours, stirring occasionally.

Yield: 3 cups

Cuisinart processor: Steel knife blade

Other processors: Attachments manufacturer recommends for chopping, and blending or pureeing

Pesto

Pesto *can be made only with fresh basil, and unfortunately the basil season is short. However, you can prepare the sauce (eliminating the cheese and butter) and freeze it for later use. When you are ready to use it, just defrost, add the cheese and butter, and serve over pasta.* Pesto *is especially fine on fettucine, cooked* al dente, *of course.*

2 firmly packed cups of basil leaves
½ cup olive oil
2 tablespoons pine, or pignolia, nuts
2 cloves garlic, each clove cut in half
1 teaspoon salt
½ cup freshly grated Parmesan cheese
3 tablespoons butter, cut into 2 or 3 pieces

Place basil, oil, nuts, garlic, and salt in food processor and puree thoroughly. Add cheese and continue blending. Add butter and blend once again. Place *pesto* sauce in a bowl, and before serving with pasta, stir in 2 tablespoons of the hot water in which the pasta has cooked.

Yield: Sauce for 4 servings of pasta

Cuisinart processor: Steel knife blade

Other processors: Blender or attachments manufacturer recommends for chopping and mixing

---

Peachy Barbecue Sauce

1 medium onion, cut in half
1 clove garlic
3 sprigs Italian parsley
Pulp of ½ lemon that has been seeded
1 six-ounce can tomato paste
¼ cup wine vinegar
½ cup water
¼ cup salad oil
2 teaspoons dry mustard
1 teaspoon soy sauce
1 teaspoon salt
1 tablespoon chili powder
1 tablespoon brown sugar
1 four-and-three-quarter-ounce jar strained baby peaches

Place first 4 ingredients in food processor and chop. Add remaining ingredients and process until smooth.

Yield: 2 cups

Cuisinart processor: Steel knife blade

Other processors: Blender or attachments manufacturer recommends for chopping and mixing

Spicy Barbecue Sauce

1 small onion, cut in half
1 clove garlic
⅓ cup vegetable oil
2 ripe tomatoes, peeled and halved
4 tablespoons chili powder
1 cup light molasses
½ cup cider vinegar
1 tablespoon Worcestershire sauce
½ teaspoon Tabasco
1 teaspoon mustard
4 teaspoons salt
1 tablespoon oregano
2 cups water

Place onion and garlic in food processor and chop. Heat oil
in a large saucepan, and sauté onion and garlic until translucent. Place tomatoes in food processor and chop. Add to
onion-garlic mixture and cook an additional 5 minutes, stirring. Add all remaining ingredients; stir to blend. Bring mixture to a boil. Lower heat and simmer uncovered for 20 to
30 minutes.

Yield: About 1 quart

Cuisinart processor: Steel knife blade

Other processors: Attachment manufacturer recommends for
  chopping

PÂTÉS

If you can make a meat loaf, then you can make a pâté or terrine—*if* you own a food processor. The problem of preparing pâtés in the past was finding a butcher willing to grind pork, pork fat, and veal in his machine. Now, with the help of a food processor, homemade pâtés can become a regular feature at your table, and they can be as simple or as elaborate as you wish.

Today there is no difference between a pâté and a terrine. Originally a pâté was a meat mixture baked in a crust; a terrine was the same mixture baked in a terrine, or earthenware dish. The terms pâté and terrine are used interchangeably.

Chicken Liver Pâté en Croûte

1 pound chicken livers, washed, dried, and cut in half
2 eggs
1 tablespoon cognac
¾ cup heavy sweet cream
1 small onion, cut in half
¼ cup all-purpose flour
2 teaspoons salt
½ teaspoon ground ginger
1 teaspoon white pepper
½ teaspoon allspice
Pâte Brisée II recipe (see page 195)
1 egg, beaten

Place livers, eggs, cognac, and cream in food processor and puree. You may have to do this in two or more steps. Add onion and flour to last batch of livers and continue pureeing. Combine entire mixture in a bowl and blend thoroughly with a fork, stirring in the seasonings. Roll out Pâte Brisée II dough and line a buttered pan that is approximately 15¾ ×2¼ × 2¾ inches. Spoon chicken liver puree into pan and fold dough over to cover the puree.

Make rosettes of scraps of dough and decorate the center of the pâté. Pierce each rosette with a sharp knife and prick casing with a fork at the edge of the pâté.

Brush dough with beaten egg and bake in a preheated 350-degree oven for approximately 45 minutes or until dough is brown.

Serves: 8

Cuisinart processor: Steel knife blade

Other processors: Blender or attachments manufacturer recommends for grinding and mixing

---

Harry's Chicken Liver Pâté

This is my husband's recipe for the ultimate chicken liver pâté. As you can see, there are few ingredients, and the result is a pâté with the richest flavor of chicken liver.

1 pound chicken livers
1 cup, or more, rendered chicken fat
1 large onion, cut into quarters
Salt to taste
Freshly ground black pepper to taste

Wash chicken livers. Cut in half, and while doing so, remove all visible bits of veins or gristle. Pat chicken livers dry with paper towels. Heat chicken fat in a large skillet. Place chicken livers in skillet and sauté until they are firm and pink inside. Place chicken livers and fat they have sautéed in, in food processor. Add onion. Process until ingredients are thoroughly pureed. You may have to do this in two or more steps. Start and stop the machine a few times, scraping puree down from sides of the bowl. Season with salt and pepper and add more chicken fat, if you wish. Spoon chicken liver pâté into a 4-cup terrine and decorate with sliced radishes. Chill at least four hours or overnight. Serve with fresh rye and caraway seed bread.

Serves: 6 to 8

Cuisinart processor: Steel knife blade

Other processors: Blender or attachments manufacturer recommends for grinding and mixing

Pâté of Chicken and Goose Liver with Mushrooms and Ham

3 tablespoons rendered goose fat, if available, or butter
1 cup mushrooms
1 small onion, cut in half
½ pound chicken livers, cut in half
1 large goose liver, cut into four pieces
¼ cup chicken stock or broth, homemade or canned
½ pound boiled ham, cut into cubes or large strips
Salt and freshly ground black pepper to taste

Heat goose fat or butter in a large skillet. Chop mushrooms and onion in food processor and place in skillet with chicken livers and goose liver. Sauté until livers have just lost their pink color. Remove all ingredients to food processor. Add chicken stock or broth, and ham. Process until all ingredients are smoothly pureed. Add salt and pepper. Spoon mixture into a 3-cup oiled terrine. Cover and refrigerate several hours or overnight. Pâté may be unmolded or served directly from terrine. Decorate with slices of hard-cooked eggs, chopped scallion, and parsley.

Serves: 6 to 8

Cuisinart processor: Steel knife blade

Other processors: Blender or attachments manufacturer recommends for grinding and mixing

PÂTÉ OF CHICKEN AND GOOSE LIVER WITH
MUSHROOMS AND HAM
Courtesy National Goose Council

Veal and Chicken Pâté en Croûte

¾ **pound boneless veal, trimmed and cut into cubes**
¾ **pound breast of chicken, boned, skinned, and cut into
   cubes**
½ **cup homemade bread crumbs**
1 **egg**
¼ **cup heavy sweet cream**
2 **tablespoons dry sherry wine**
¼ **pound mushrooms, washed and cut in half**
¼ **teaspoon tarragon**
3 **sprigs parsley**
1 **tablespoon fresh, or dried, chives**
½ **teaspoon salt**
Pâte Brisée I (French pastry dough, see page 194)
1 **beaten egg**

Place meat in food processor and grind. You may have to do
this in two steps. Turn machine on and off and push meat down
from the sides of the bowl, if necessary. When meat is ground,
add all other ingredients to processor except pâte brisée and
beaten egg. Blend thoroughly. Again, you may have to do this
final blending in two steps.

Spoon meat mixture into a buttered 8½ × 4½ × 2½ loaf pan.
Bake in a preheated 350-degree oven for 1 hour. Allow meat
mixture to cool and then remove from pan.

Make pâte brisée according to directions on page 194. Roll out
the dough and place cooled loaf in center. Fold dough over
the meat to cover it completely. Tuck in dough at the edges.

Place seam side down on a baking sheet. Make rosettes out of scraps of dough and decorate the center of the pâté. Pierce each rosette with a sharp knife, and prick dough casing with a fork at the edges of the pâté. Brush dough with beaten egg and bake in a preheated 400-degree oven for approximately 40 minutes or until crust is brown.

Serves: 8

Cuisinart processor: Steel knife blade

Other processors: Attachments manufacturer recommends for grinding and mixing

ჂჂჂ

Country-Style Terrine
from Au Relais Hostellerie

It was our good fortune to be taken through the château country of France's Loire Valley by our French friends Batia, Artur, Raymonde, and Theo. Along the way, we stopped at a small country inn, Au Relais Hostellerie, in Bracieux, where we had a meal that the resident of any castle might have envied. The first course was a terrine, which the owner and chef of this marvelous inn described as "the usual country-style pâté —nothing special." It tasted very special to us, and I think it will to you, too.

½ **pound pork, boned, trimmed, and cut into cubes**
½ **pound fresh pork fat, cut into pieces**
½ **pound breast of chicken, skinned, boned, and cut into cubes**
Salt and freshly ground black pepper to taste
½ **teaspoon thyme**
2 cloves garlic
1 small onion
4 tablespoons cognac
2 eggs
½ **pound pork liver, cut into large chunks**
Sheets of fresh pork fat, about ⅛ inch thick, to line terrine

Place pork, pork fat, chicken, salt, pepper, thyme, garlic, and onions in food processor and grind. Add cognac and eggs and continue blending. You may have to do this in two or more steps. Sauté a tablespoonful of mixture in a skillet to taste and correct seasoning. Spoon mixture into a large bowl. Place pork liver in food processor and chop coarsely. Stir chopped pork liver into mixture in bowl. Line bottom and sides of a 6-cup terrine or loaf pan with sheets of pork fat and spoon mixture into terrine. Cover mixture with another sheet of pork fat. Make sure that the fat is tucked in on sides and at the ends so mixture is completely covered. Seal the entire pan with foil. Set terrine in a larger pan of water, and place in a preheated oven of 350 degrees. Bake approximately 2 hours. Pâté is cooked when meat shrinks from sides of terrine or loaf pan in which it is cooking. Test for doneness by pressing top of pâté with a spoon. There should be no traces of pink in juices. Or you can test by piercing the center with a metal skewer. Skewer should come out clean.

Remove pâté from oven. Place another pan on top of pâté, and place a weight within this pan. Pâté should be weighted down as it cools, so that excess fat is pressed out and pâté is easier to slice. When pâté has cooled, refrigerate, with the weight still on. Be sure not to pour off any of the cooking juices.

Serve pâté only after it is thoroughly chilled. You may serve right from the terrine.

Serves: 12 to 14

Cuisinart processor: Steel knife blade

Other processors: Attachments manufacturer recommends for grinding and chopping

Sausage Pâté en Croûte

1 small onion
3 shallots
2 scallions, each one cut into 3 pieces
6 slices bacon
2 pounds pork sausage meat
3 eggs
3 cups homemade bread crumbs
Salt and freshly ground black pepper to taste
¼ teaspoon thyme
2 tablespoons cognac
All-American Pie Crust Dough (see page 198, and double the recipe)
1 beaten egg

Place onion, shallots, and scallions in food processor and chop. Leave vegetables in processor. In a large skillet fry the bacon. When bacon is crisp, remove from heat and combine with sausage meat. Add bacon, sausage meat, eggs, and bread crumbs to food processor. Blend thoroughly. You may have to do this in two or more steps. Season sausage mixture, add cognac, and sauté a tablespoon of mixture in a skillet. Taste, and correct seasoning. Line a 5-cup terrine or loaf pan with rolled-out pie crust dough. Spoon mixture into terrine, bringing pie crust dough over top of sausage mixture. Brush with beaten egg. Bake terrine in a preheated 350-degree oven for 45 minutes. Invert pan on a flat plate and refrigerate overnight. Slide loaf from pan the following day.

Serves: 8

Cuisinart processor: Steel knife blade

Other processors: Attachments manufacturer recommends for grinding and mixing

---

Jellied Ham Pâté

3 shallots, peeled and minced
2 tablespoons sweet butter
1 cup chicken broth, homemade or canned
1 canned pimiento
1 stalk celery, cut into 3 pieces
½ green pepper, cut into 2 pieces
¼ pound boiled ham, cut into cubes or strips
1 teaspoon Dijon mustard
2 tablespoons tomato paste
2 tablespoons cognac
1 envelope unflavored gelatin softened in 2 tablespoons dry vermouth
Salt and freshly ground black pepper to taste
½ cup heavy sweet cream, whipped

Place shallots and butter in a saucepan and cook until shallots are translucent. Stir in chicken broth, bring to a simmer, and reserve.

Place pimiento, celery, green pepper, and ham in food processor and process until all ingredients are finely chopped and blended. You may have to do this in two or more steps.

Add shallot-chicken broth mixture, mustard, tomato paste, and cognac to processor and blend thoroughly. You may have to do this in two or more steps.

Add gelatin-wine mixture to processor and blend thoroughly. Spoon mixture from processor into a large bowl and add seasonings. Fold in whipped cream and spoon pâté into a 4-cup buttered mold. Chill overnight or until set.

Serves: 6

Cuisinart processor: Steel knife blade

Other processors: Blender or attachments manufacturer recommends for grinding and mixing

Chicken Pâté Romanoff

1 shallot, minced
1 clove garlic, minced
4 tablespoons butter
1 pound veal, boned, trimmed, and cut into cubes
5 chicken legs, skinned and boned, the meat cut into pieces
1½ cups homemade bread crumbs
1 egg
½ tablespoon mild paprika
**½ teaspoon Herbes de Provence (or ¼ teaspoon thyme
  and ¼ bay leaf, crushed)**
3 tablespoons Italian parsley
½ cup dry white wine
¼ cup brandy

Sauté shallot and garlic in butter until translucent. Place in food processor with butter in which vegetables have sautéed. Add all other ingredients to processor and blend thoroughly. You may have to do this in two steps, mixing contents finally in a large bowl. Spoon pâté mixture into a buttered 5-cup terrine or loaf pan. Set pan in a larger one that's partially filled with water and bake in a preheated 350-degree oven for 1 hour and 30 minutes.

Serves: 8 to 10

Cuisinart processor: Steel knife blade

Other processors: Attachments manufacturer recommends
  for grinding and mixing

MEATS

The food processor is an absolute must for all kinds of ground-meat dishes. Whether you like a well-done hamburger or a raw Steak Tartare, the processor will grind meat for these and other favorites in seconds. Freshly ground chopped meat has a flavor and texture far superior to that of meat that has been ground at the supermarket.

Most butchers are reluctant to chop anything other than beef in their grinders. With your own food processor you can easily prepare meat loaves and meatballs made with chopped pork and veal and Middle Eastern dishes made with chopped lamb. And now that you can grind your own meats, you can be absolutely certain of the contents of every dish you serve.

The food processor also solves the leftover meat problem. Instead of shifting yesterday's turkey or roast beef from one refrigerator shelf to another, you can grind the meat in the processor and combine it with vegetables or a freshly prepared sauce to create new and exciting meals.

Vitello Tonnato

Vitello Tonnato *has long been a favorite among people who like fine Italian food, but many preferred to eat it in restaurants rather than prepare it at home. It simply took too much time and trouble to puree the Tuna Sauce through a sieve or strainer. It's no trouble now, thanks to the food processor.*

Serve Vitello Tonnato *with a first course of small black olives, pimientos, slices of mortadella, and crisp, thin bread sticks. Prepare a romaine and escarole salad and serve a dry white Italian wine.*

2 tablespoons olive oil
3 pounds boneless rolled leg of veal
1 large onion, cut into quarters
2 carrots, each one cut into 3 pieces
3 stalks celery, each one cut into 3 pieces
2 cloves garlic
3 sprigs Italian parsley
1 two-ounce can anchovy fillets
1 seven-ounce can tuna fish, drained
1 cup dry white wine
1 cup chicken broth, homemade or canned
¼ teaspoon oregano
Salt and freshly ground black pepper to taste
1 cup homemade mayonnaise
1 tablespoon lemon juice, or more, to taste

Heat oil in a large Dutch oven and brown veal lightly on all sides. Place onion, carrots, celery, garlic, and parsley in food processor and chop. Add to veal along with anchovy, tuna, wine, broth, oregano, and salt and pepper. Cover Dutch oven and cook for 1½ to 2 hours or until veal is tender. Remove meat from Dutch oven and chill.

Reduce the sauce by one half, and return to food processor; blend thoroughly. Chill sauce, blend in mayonnaise, and add lemon juice to taste.

When veal is chilled, cut into thin slices and serve with the sauce.

Serves: 6 to 8

Cuisinart processor: Steel knife blade

Other processors: Blender or attachments manufacturer recommends for chopping and mixing

❊ʃ❊ʃ❊ʃ❊

Beef Wellington

Filet of beef, rolled in a pastry crust, is a most impressive dinner or party dish. Some cooks use a many-layered puff pastry or a brioche dough for Beef Wellington, but a Pâte Brisée made without sugar turns out a delicious crust.

Pâte Brisée II (double the recipe on page 195)
1 two-and-a-half- to three-pound filet of beef
3 tablespoons cognac
Salt and freshly ground black pepper to taste
8 strips bacon
½ pound Chicken Liver Pâté (one half the recipe on page 83)
1 egg, beaten

Prepare Pâte Brisée II, doubling the recipe on page 195. Depending on your processor, you may have to do this in two steps. Chill dough for 30 to 45 minutes before using.

Preheat oven to 450 degrees. Rub the filet with the cognac, season with salt and pepper, and place filet in a roasting pan. Place bacon strips over top of meat.

Roast filet for 15 minutes. Remove filet from oven. Discard bacon and allow meat to cool to room temperature.

Spread Chicken Liver Pâté over filet.

Preheat oven to 425 degrees.

Roll out Pâte Brisée dough and place filet in the center. Draw dough up from both sides so that it overlaps, and tuck in ends of dough envelope-fashion, trimming off excess dough.

Seal all pastry seams with beaten egg and place pastry-wrapped filet on a baking sheet, seam side down.

Brush top and sides of filet with remaining beaten egg. Make rosettes out of dough scraps and decorate top of filet with rosettes. Pierce center of each rosette with a sharp knife and prick pastry casing on top and sides.

Place filet in oven and bake for approximately 30 minutes or until pastry is cooked and has browned.

Serves: 6 to 8

Cuisinart processor: Steel knife blade for pastry and pâté

Other processors: Dough hook or other attachment manufacturer recommends for kneading; blender for pâté or other
attachment manufacturer recommends for grinding and
mixing

❋∫❋∫❋∫❋

Meat Loaf with Water Chestnuts

1 pound beef, trimmed and cubed
½ pound veal, trimmed and cubed
½ pound lean pork, trimmed and cubed
2 eggs
2 ounces instant oatmeal
6–8 canned water chestnuts, drained
½ green pepper, cut into 2 pieces
1 small onion, cut in half
3 tablespoons ketchup
1 teaspoon salt
½ teaspoon freshly ground black pepper

Place meat in food processor and grind. You may have to do this in two or more steps. Add eggs and oatmeal to last batch of meat and continue processing until well blended. Place meat, egg, and oatmeal mixture in a large bowl.

Place water chestnuts, green pepper, and onion in processor and chop coarsely. Add to meat mixture. Stir in ketchup, salt, and pepper and mix thoroughly, using a large fork.

Form meat into a loaf shape and place in the center of a shallow roasting pan or baking dish. Place in a preheated 350-degree oven and bake for an hour and a half.

May be served with Tomato Sauce (see page 76).

Serves: 8

Cuisinart processor: Steel knife blade

Other processors: Attachments manufacturer recommends for grinding, chopping, and mixing

MEAT LOAF WITH WATER CHESTNUTS
Courtesy National Livestock & Meat Board

Meat Loaf

. **1 pound beef, trimmed and cut into cubes**
3 slices white bread, halved, crusts trimmed
1 eight-ounce can stewed tomatoes
1 egg
1 teaspoon salt
1 envelope dried onion soup mix
½ teaspoon freshly ground black pepper
2 sprigs parsley
2 slices American cheese
4 slices bacon

Place beef in food processor and grind. You may have to do this in two or more steps. Add all other ingredients, except cheese and bacon, to processor. Blend thoroughly.

Form one half of meat mixture into a loaf. Place cheese slices on top of meat. Cover cheese with remaining meat mixture, making sure that cheese is completely sealed in at the sides. Top meat mixture with bacon strips. Preheat oven to 350 degrees and bake for 1 hour or until well browned.

Serves: 6

Cuisinart processor: Steel knife blade

Other processors: Attachments manufacturer recommends for grinding and mixing

Home-Style Italian Meatballs

½ **pound beef, trimmed and cut into cubes**
¼ **pound pork, trimmed and cut into cubes**
¼ **pound veal, trimmed and cut into cubes**
4 sprigs Italian parsley
1 egg
1 small onion, cut in half
2 cloves garlic
4 slices white bread, halved, crusts trimmed
1 teaspoon salt
⅛ **teaspoon freshly ground black pepper**
¼ **teaspoon oregano**
½ **cup olive oil**

Place beef, pork, and veal in food processor and grind. You may have to do this in two or more steps. Add all other ingredients, except oil, to meat, and continue processing until mixture is thoroughly mixed. This may also require two or more steps. Turn the machine on and off as you process, scraping meat down from sides of the bowl.

When mixture is combined, form into meatballs, approximately 2 inches in diameter. Heat olive oil in a large skillet and fry meatballs until they are brown. (If you wish, instead of frying, you may cook meatballs for 1 hour in your favorite marinara sauce and serve over spaghetti.)

Serves: 6

Cuisinart processor: Steel knife blade

Other processors: Attachments manufacturer recommends for grinding and mixing

Swedish Meatballs

½ pound beef, trimmed and cut into cubes
¼ pound veal, trimmed and cut into cubes
¼ pound pork, trimmed and cut into cubes
4 slices of white bread, cut in half, crusts trimmed
1 large onion, cut into quarters
4 sprigs Italian parsley
1 clove garlic
2 eggs
1 cup sweet cream
1 teaspoon salt
1 tablespoon fresh dill
Freshly ground black pepper to taste
¼ pound, or more, sweet butter
1 ten-and-a-half-ounce can condensed onion soup
½ cup water
¼ cup beer
¼ cup ketchup
1 tablespoon flour
½ cup sour cream

Place meat in food processor and grind. You may have to do this in two or more steps. Remove meat from processor. Place bread, onion, parsley, and garlic in processor; add eggs, cream, salt, dill, and pepper and process until well mixed, about 10 seconds. You may have to do this in two or more steps. Combine with meat.

Form meat mixture into meatballs approximately two inches in diameter. Heat butter in a large skillet and brown meatballs. Remove meatballs to another dish and add onion soup, water, beer, and ketchup to skillet. Bring to a simmer. Combine flour

SWEDISH MEATBALLS
Courtesy National Livestock & Meat Board

and sour cream in a small bowl, mixing well, and add gradually to skillet. Simmer sauce for about 10 minutes. Add meatballs to skillet and heat for another 5 minutes. Serve with wide buttered egg noodles.

Serves: 6

Cuisinart processor: Steel knife blade

Other processors: Attachments manufacturer recommends for grinding and mixing

Ham Loaf in Potato Crust

HAM LOAF INGREDIENTS

1½ pounds cooked ham, cut into cubes
½ pound Italian sausage, casing removed, cut into slices
2 slices canned pineapple, cut in half
1 tablespoon soy sauce
2 teaspoons Dijon mustard
2 eggs
4 slices white bread, crusts trimmed, cut into quarters
3 sprigs parsley
1 medium onion, cut in half
½ green pepper, cut into two pieces

Place ham in food processor and grind. You may have to do this in two or more steps. Remove and reserve. Place all other ingredients in processor and grind. Add ham to processor and blend all ingredients thoroughly. Process by turning machine on and off and pushing mixture down from sides of bowl. You may have to do this in two or more steps. Spoon ham loaf mixture into a buttered 9×5×3-inch loaf pan. Bake in a pre-heated 350-degree oven for an hour and fifteen minutes.

Cuisinart processor: Steel knife blade

Other processors: Attachments manufacturer recommends
  for grinding and mixing

POTATO CRUST INGREDIENTS

1 pound potatoes, peeled, cubed, boiled, and drained
1 three-ounce package cream cheese, cut into 3 pieces
¼ pound Cheddar cheese, cut into cubes
2 tablespoons sweet butter
2 tablespoons milk
1 tablespoon dried chives
¼ teaspoon salt
¼ teaspoon white pepper
Mild paprika

Place boiled, drained potatoes in food processor and puree until smooth. Add remaining ingredients, except paprika, and continue processing until smooth. You may have to do this in two or more steps.

Cuisinart processor: Steel knife blade

Other processors: Attachments manufacturer recommends for beating and mixing

Assembling Ham Loaf and Potato Crust:

Turn baked Ham Loaf onto baking sheet. Spread potato mixture over loaf. If desired, you can decorate ham loaf on top by piping part of potato mixture through a pastry tube. Sprinkle top of loaf with paprika. Bake in 400-degree oven for 20 minutes.

Serves: 6

Rotisserie Flank Steak

1 flank steak, 2–2½ pounds
Salt and freshly ground black pepper to taste
2 tablespoons butter
1 large Spanish onion, cut into 4 pieces
6 sprigs Italian parsley
1 cup dry red wine
¼ cup dark molasses
2 cloves garlic, each one cut into 4 pieces

Sprinkle flank steak with salt and pepper and set aside. Heat butter in a skillet. Place onion and parsley in food processor and chop. Add chopped onion and parsley to hot butter and sauté until onions are translucent. Spread flank steak with onion-parsley mixture. Starting at narrow end, roll up steak and tie with string. Skewer ends of roll to keep stuffing inside meat.

Make a marinade by combining wine, molasses, and garlic. Pour over meat, which has been placed in a glass or earthenware dish. Let stand 4 to 8 hours.

To cook: Place meat on a rotisserie skewer, making sure that it is properly balanced for easy turning. Roast meat about 6 inches from gray coals. Brush with marinade every 10 to 15 minutes. Roast for about 1 hour or until meat is tender. Remove from skewer and cut into 1-inch slices.

Serves: 6

Cuisinart processor: Steel knife blade

Other processors: Blender or attachment manufacturer recommends for chopping

Crispy Hash Pancake

1 pound, or more, of leftover roast beef, cut into cubes
1 large onion, cut into quarters
1 green pepper, cored, seeded, and cut into 4 pieces
4 large Idaho potatoes, cut into cubes and boiled
¼ cup ketchup
Salt and freshly ground black pepper to taste

Place roast beef, onion, and green pepper in food processor and chop. You may have to do this in two or more steps. Remove beef mixture to a large bowl and add potatoes and seasoning; mash together with a large fork. Do not add the potatoes to the meat in the food processor, because potatoes will become finely processed and the texture of this hash will be too smooth.

Spread hash mixture in a thin layer over a lightly greased or teflon-coated baking pan or baking sheet, and place in a pre-heated 450-degree oven. Bake until hash is very brown and crispy. Depending on your oven, this can take anywhere from 20 to 40 minutes. Serve in large wedges with a sliced tomato and onion salad.

Serves: 4 to 6

Cuisinart processor: Steel knife blade

Other processors: Attachment manufacturer recommends for grinding

Steak Tartare

We've discovered that more people are developing a taste for raw beef. Years ago, when we served this dish, people would edge away from the table. Now we find more people heading for the platter holding the Steak Tartare. The essential ingredient in this dish is freshness. The spices and herbs can be varied to suit your taste. After you prepare the basic meat mixture, you can add extra capers, mustard, or hot sauce.

1 pound beef, cut into cubes (may be round, sirloin, or filet, but must be absolutely fat free)
1 whole egg
1 small onion, cut in half
2 tablespoons olive oil
Salt and freshly ground black pepper to taste
1 teaspoon Worcestershire sauce, or more, to taste
⅛ teaspoon Tabasco, or more, to taste
1 teaspoon Dijon mustard, or more, to taste
1 tablespoon ketchup, or more, to taste
1 tablespoon capers

Place meat, egg, onion, and olive oil in food processor and grind. You may have to do this in two or more steps. Remove meat to a large bowl and stir in other ingredients. When serving, you can have additional small bowls of capers, chopped parsley, and chopped onions for your guests who may wish them.

Serve with triangular slices of black bread.

Serves: 4 to 6

Cuisinart processor: Steel knife blade

Other processors: Attachments manufacturer recommends for grinding

---

Steak Tartare and Caviar

If you serve Steak Tartare with caviar, you can leave out the seasonings, because caviar is all the seasoning you need. You don't have to buy Beluga or Sevruga, as whitefish roe seasons marvelously. Lumpfish roe, while fine for other dishes, will not do for this one, so be sure to read the label on all caviar jars carefully.

> **1 pound beef, cut into cubes (may be round, sirloin, or fillet, but must be absolutely fat free)**
> **8 ounces of black caviar (whitefish roe may be used)**
> **1 onion, cut into quarters**
> **Buttered toast halves, made from thinly cut white bread, crusts trimmed**

Place meat in food processor and grind. You may have to do this in two or more steps. Pile ground meat into your loveliest bowl or dish. Set jar of caviar in a bowl filled with cracked ice and place beside ground meat. Place onion in food processor and chop finely. Spoon onion into a small dish and place beside meat and caviar. Wrap buttered toast in a white linen napkin and add to array surrounding the meat. Let guests help themselves to toast, which they will spread with meat and top with caviar and a sprinkling of onion. Serve with champagne or vodka.

Serves: 4 to 6

Cuisinart processor: Steel knife blade

Other processors: Attachments manufacturer recommends for grinding and chopping

Texas Tacos

TACO SHELLS

1 cup flour
⅓ cup cornmeal
½ teaspoon salt
2 tablespoons shortening
¼ to ½ cup warm water

Place flour, cornmeal, salt, and shortening in food processor. Blend until shortening is cut into flour mixture. Add water and blend until dough forms a ball. Cover and refrigerate for at least 1 hour. Form dough into 10 small balls. Roll out on a lightly floured board to 6-inch diameter.

Fry tacos on a very lightly greased hot griddle or in a frying pan, for approximately 1 to 2 minutes on each side or until tacos are dry and lightly browned. Fold in half immediately upon removing from fry pan.

Yield: 10 Taco shells

Cuisinart processor: Steel knife blade

Other processors: Dough hook or attachments manufacturer recommends for kneading

TACO FILLING AND TOPPING

1½ pounds beef, trimmed and cut into cubes
1 small onion
1 clove garlic
3 sprigs parsley
2 tablespoons oil
2 tablespoons chili powder
2 teaspoons ground cumin
½ teaspoon salt
¼ teaspoon celery seed
¼ teaspoon dried basil
1 six-ounce can tomato paste
1 cup water
1 cup grated Cheddar cheese
1 cup shredded lettuce
½ cup chopped onion
1 tomato, diced

Place meat, onion, garlic, and parsley in food processor and grind. You may have to do this in two or more steps. Heat oil in a large skillet and fry meat mixture until lightly browned. Add chili powder, cumin, salt, celery seed, basil, tomato paste, and water to skillet and simmer, stirring for 15 minutes.

Cuisinart processor: Steel knife blade

Other processors: Attachment manufacturer recommends for grinding

Assembling Texas Tacos:

Fill each taco shell with meat mixture and top with grated cheese, shredded lettuce, chopped onion, and diced tomato, which have been processed separately in food processor.

Serves: 5

Kibbeh Nayé

Kibbeh, *in all its variations, is a favorite dish throughout the Mideast. This recipe, made with raw lamb, may surprise many non-Mideasterners, who find themselves addicted to* kibbeh nayé *once they taste it.*

1 pound lamb, cubed, trimmed, and absolutely fat free (leg of lamb is best)
Salt and freshly ground black pepper to taste
1 large onion, cut into quarters
1 cup fine bulgur, or cracked wheat
Lemon quarters
Lettuce leaves

Place meat, salt, pepper, and onion in food processor and grind until meat is smooth and pastelike. You may have to do this in two or more steps. Place bulgur in a strainer, and rinse. Squeeze out water by hand and then add bulgur to meat mixture in processor. Process, turning machine on and off and scraping mixture down from sides of bowl until *kibbeh* is absolutely smooth. Spoon *kibbeh* onto lettuce leaves and serve with lemon quarters. You may also serve a bread basket of sesame crackers or pita bread along with the *kibbeh*.

Serves: 4 to 6

Cuisinart processor: Steel knife blade

Other processors: Attachments manufacturer recommends for grinding; put meat mixture through twice, and meat-bulgur mixture at least twice more.

Lamb-Stuffed Zucchini

4 medium to large zucchini
1 pound lamb, trimmed and cut into cubes
1 medium onion, cut into quarters
¼ cup olive oil
1 cup cooked rice
Salt and freshly ground black pepper to taste
1 one-pound can stewed whole tomatoes, drained
2 teaspoons sugar, or more, to taste
¼ teaspoon hot paprika
⅛ teaspoon hot pepper flakes (optional)

Peel zucchini and parboil until vegetable is barely tender, about 10 to 15 minutes. Remove zucchini from water and let cool.

Place meat and onion in food processor and grind. You may have to do this in two or more steps. Heat oil in a large skillet and sauté meat-onion mixture until lightly brown. Stir in cooked rice and season with salt and pepper.

Cut cooled zucchini in half, scoop out centers, and discard. Fill zucchini halves with meat-rice mixture and place in baking dish. If there's any of the meat-rice mixture left, distribute it around the stuffed vegetables.

Place stewed tomatoes in processor and chop coarsely. Season to taste with sugar, paprika, and hot pepper flakes and pour over stuffed zucchini. Place baking dish in a preheated 350-degree oven and bake for 30 to 40 minutes.

Serves: 4 to 6

Cuisinart processor: Steel knife blade

Other processors: Attachments manufacturer recommends for grinding and chopping

Turkey Mousse San Francisco

1 head iceberg lettuce
1 cup turkey or chicken broth, homemade or canned
2 cups cooked turkey, cut into cubes
1 small onion
1 cup homemade mayonnaise
2 tablespoons lemon juice
¾ teaspoon salt
3 envelopes gelatin
½ cup water
1 cup heavy sweet cream for whipping
2 cups whole cranberry sauce (optional)

Core, rinse, and thoroughly drain lettuce. Place lettuce in food processor and shred enough for two tightly packed cups of shredded lettuce. After measuring, return shredded lettuce to processor and add broth. Process until thoroughly blended. Add turkey, onion, mayonnaise, lemon juice, and salt. Process until completely smooth. You may have to do this in two or more steps.

Mix gelatin and water. Heat, stirring, until gelatin is completely dissolved. In a bowl, blend gelatin into turkey mixture. Chill until mixture mounds softly on a spoon.

Whip cream until stiff. Using a spoon, fold whipped cream into turkey mixture. Turn into a 6-cup mold and chill until firm. Unmold onto a serving platter and garnish with lettuce and cranberry sauce.

TURKEY MOUSSE SAN FRANCISCO
Courtesy Western Iceberg Lettuce, Inc.

Serves: 8

Cuisinart processor: Shredding disc for lettuce; steel knife blade for all other ingredients

Other processors: Attachments manufacturer recommends for shredding, grinding, and whipping

Turkey is low in calories, high in protein, and when it's not Thanksgiving, it's an especially good buy at most supermarkets. Here are two tasty recipes using turkey and pears. Both are easy to prepare, thanks to the food processor.

Turkey Burgers with Fruit Glaze

1 pound of raw turkey meat, trimmed and cut into chunks
3 Bartlett pears
1 small onion
Salt to taste
½ teaspoon poultry seasoning
¼ cup quick-cooking oats
1 egg
¼ to ½ cup flour
¼ pound margarine
1 cup cranberry juice cocktail
2 teaspoons cornstarch
2 teaspoons soy sauce

Place chunks of turkey in food processor and grind. You may have to do this in two or more steps. You should have about 2½ cups of ground meat. Peel, core, and halve one pear and add to turkey meat in food processor, along with onion, salt, poultry seasoning, oats, and egg. Blend thoroughly. Remove mixture from processor and form into 6 burgers. Roll burgers lightly in flour.

Heat margarine in a deep skillet and brown burgers on both sides. Cover skillet and continue cooking burgers over low heat for 30 to 40 minutes or until turkey is tender.

Before serving, beat together cranberry juice and cornstarch in a small bowl, making sure there are no lumps. Pour over burgers in skillet, mixing well with pan juices. Stir over low heat until glaze is bubbling and has thickened slightly.

Peel, core, and slice the two remaining pears and add to skillet. Stir in soy sauce. Allow glaze to simmer for two more minutes and serve.

Serves: 6

Cuisinart processor: Steel knife blade

Other processors: Attachments manufacturer recommends for grinding and mixing

ᏧᏧᏧ

Turkey 'n' Pear Chili

½ pound raw turkey meat, cut into chunks
1 small onion
1 clove garlic
1 tablespoon oil
Salt and freshly ground black pepper to taste
1 teaspoon chili powder
1 teaspoon sugar
½ teaspoon mild paprika
Dash of cayenne pepper
1 one-pound can stewed tomatoes
1 teaspoon lemon juice
2 large Bartlett pears
1 teaspoon cornstarch
½ cup water

Place meat, onion, and garlic clove in food processor and grind. Heat oil in a large skillet. Add contents of processor to skillet and brown. Add seasonings to meat mixture and continue cooking for another 2 minutes. Place tomatoes in food processor and chop coarsely. Add tomatoes and lemon juice to mixture in skillet and simmer for fifteen minutes, stirring occasionally.

Peel, halve, and core the two pears. Set aside. Blend cornstarch and water and stir into mixture in skillet. Bring to a boil and cook 1 more minute. Spoon meat mixture into pear halves and serve.

Serves: 4

Cuisinart processor: Steel knife blade

Other processors: Attachments manufacturer recommends for grinding and chopping

---

TURKEY 'N' PEAR CHILI
Courtesy California Tree Fruit Agreement

Chicken Apple Curry Sikander

1 tablespoon curry powder
2 tablespoons sweet butter
1 medium onion, cut in half
1 clove garlic
2 tablespoons flour
2 cups chicken broth, homemade or canned
2 Macintosh apples, cored and cut in half
3 cups cooked chicken, cut into pieces
Salt and freshly ground black pepper to taste

Sauté curry powder in butter in a large skillet over low heat for 2 to 3 minutes. Place onion and garlic in food processor and chop. Add chopped onion, garlic, and flour to skillet and sauté, stirring until flour is lightly browned. Stir in broth and continue simmering until sauce thickens. Place apples and chicken in food processor and chop coarsely. You may have to do this in two or more steps. Add chicken-apple mixture to sauce. Season to taste.

Serve with cooked rice and such curry relishes as chutney, grated coconut, salted nuts, grated lemon rind, and poppadums.

Serves: 3 to 4

Cuisinart processor: Steel knife blade

Other processors: Attachment manufacturer recommends for chopping

Chicken Croquettes

½ pound cooked chicken, cut into cubes
1 large boiled potato, cut into quarters
1 small onion, cut into 2 pieces
2 sprigs parsley
4 mushrooms
½ carrot, cut into 2 pieces
1 stalk celery, cut into 3 pieces
1 egg
4 slices white bread, crusts trimmed, cut into quarters
½ cup light cream
1 teaspoon salt
½ teaspoon white pepper
¼ cup flour
½ cup homemade bread crumbs
Vegetable oil

Place chicken in processor and grind. Remove and reserve. Place all other ingredients in processor, except bread crumbs and oil, and blend thoroughly. Add ground chicken gradually to ingredients in processor and process until thoroughly blended. You may have to do this in two or more steps. Form chicken mixture into ovals and roll in bread crumbs. Heat oil in a large skillet and fry croquettes until golden brown. Serve with a cream sauce or a cheese sauce.

Serves: 4 to 6

Cuisinart processor: Steel knife blade

Other processors: Attachments manufacturer recommends for grinding and mixing

FISH
AND
SHELLFISH

The most complicated fish dish can grace your table this evening, thanks to the food processor. Fish quenelles, those delicate dumplings made from a forcemeat of fish, are now easy to prepare. No need to press fish through a fine sieve or work away with a mortar and pestle. Your food processor will do all the work in seconds. And this is just one of the ways you can use the food processor in the preparation of fish and shellfish.

You will find a variety of fish dishes in this chapter. Some, such as Fish Mousse, will provide an epicurean delight for your next dinner party. Others, such as Fish Hash, make tasty use of leftovers for a simple family meal. With your food processor you can soon become an expert at preparing a myriad of wonderful fish and shellfish dishes.

Fried Clam Fritters

1 pint fresh clams, out of the shell, cleaned, and drained
2 eggs
⅓ cup milk
1 cup flour
2 teaspoons baking powder
Salt and freshly ground black pepper to taste
2 cups oil

Place clams in food processor and chop coarsely. Add all other ingredients, except oil, to food processor and blend.

Heat oil in a large skillet and drop tablespoonfuls of fritter mixture into hot oil. Fry until fritters are brown on both sides, about 3 to 5 minutes. Remove with slotted spoon and drain on paper towels. Serve with tartar sauce and a large tossed salad.

Serves: 6

Cuisinart processor: Steel knife blade

Other processors: Attachments manufacturer recommends for chopping and mixing

Spicy Creole Crab Cakes

1 pound cooked crab meat, picked over to remove all bits of cartilage
¼ small onion
1 egg
1 cup homemade bread crumbs
1 teaspoon dry mustard
Dash of cayenne pepper
¼ cup, or more, milk
4 tablespoons flour
¼ pound sweet butter

Place crab meat in food processor and grind. Add all remaining ingredients, except flour and butter, and blend thoroughly. You may have to do this in two steps. Form crab meat mixture into flat cakes. Roll lightly in flour. Heat butter in a large skillet and fry crab cakes until they are brown on both sides.

Serves: 4

Cuisinart processor: Steel knife blade

Other processors: Attachments manufacturer recommends for grinding and mixing

Gefilte Fish, fish balls
poached in stock

3 pounds filleted fish (may be carp, whitefish, or a combination of both) cut into chunks
3 medium onions, cut into quarters
2 eggs
1 teaspoon salt
½ teaspoon white pepper
½ cup homemade bread crumbs or ½ cup Matzo Meal

INGREDIENTS FOR STOCK

1 onion, cut in half
3 carrots
5 sprigs parsley
heads, skin, and bones of fish
Salt and freshly ground pepper

Place filleted fish chunks in food processor and grind. You may have to do this in two or more steps. Add quartered onions, eggs, salt, pepper, and bread crumbs or matzo meal and continue processing until very smooth. Again, the processing may have to be done in two or more steps, and the final assembling can be accomplished in a large bowl. Form fish mixture into small balls.

Prepare stock by slicing onion and carrots and placing in a large saucepan. Add parsley; heads, skin, and bones of fish; and salt and freshly ground pepper. Cover with at least 1 quart of water and bring stock to a boil. Simmer for 15 minutes and then add fish balls. Add water, if necessary, to cover. Keep stock at a simmer, cover pot, and cook 2 hours. Remove gefilte fish balls from stock. Strain stock and pour around fish balls. Serve when chilled.

Serves: 6 to 8

Cuisinart processor: Steel knife blade

Other processors: Attachments manufacturer recommends for grinding and mixing

✻♪✻♪✻

Magda's Fish Salad

1 onion, cut in half
3 stalks celery, leaves and all, cut in half
2 tablespoons vinegar
A few red pepper flakes
2 carrots, cut in half
Salt and freshly ground black pepper to taste
4 pounds halibut fillets
2 stalks celery, each cut into 3 pieces
2 green peppers, each seeded, cored, and cut into 3 or 4 pieces
2 cups homemade mayonnaise
Salt and freshly ground black pepper to taste

Place first 6 ingredients in a large pot or fish poacher with 2 quarts of water. Bring water to a boil and continue boiling for 20 minutes. Reduce heat until water simmers, and slip halibut fillets into this *court-bouillon*. Poach fish until fork pierces the fish easily. Depending on the thickness of the fillets, this can take anywhere from 10 to 20 minutes. Remove fish from bouillon and allow to cool.

Cut fish into large pieces and place in food processor. Chop coarsely. You may have to do this in two or more steps. Remove fish to a large bowl. Place celery and green peppers in processor and chop coarsely. Add to fish, along with mayonnaise and seasonings. Stir with a large spoon and pile into your prettiest glass bowl. Chill at least 4 hours before serving.

Serves: 8

Cuisinart processor: Steel knife blade

Other processors: Attachment manufacturer recommends for chopping

New England Fish Hash

1 pound cooked fillet of cod or halibut, cut into chunks
4 potatoes, cubed, boiled, and drained
1 small onion
¼ pound salt pork, cut into cubes
Salt and freshly ground black pepper to taste

Place fish chunks in food processor and chop. Add potatoes and onion and process until mixture is blended. You may have to do this in two or more steps.

Render salt pork in a large skillet. Remove scraps and leave fat in pan. Spoon fish mixture from processor into skillet and stir until thoroughly heated. Continue cooking until mixture is well browned. Fold hash as you would an omelet and serve.

Serves: 4

Cuisinart processor: Steel knife blade

Other processors: Attachments manufacturer recommends for chopping and mixing

Quenelles de Poisson et Sauce aux Crevettes et Vin

1 pound fillet of flounder, sole, or salmon, cut into chunks
1 cup water
4 tablespoons sweet butter
¼ teaspoon salt
½ cup flour
2 eggs
3 sprigs parsley
4 mushrooms
1 small onion
3 tablespoons heavy sweet cream

Place fish in food processor and grind until smooth. You may have to do this in two or more steps. Remove and reserve ground fish.

Combine water and butter in a small saucepan and bring to a boil. Quickly stir in salt and all the flour. Stir with a wooden spoon and cook over a low heat for approximately 2 minutes or until mixture coats the bottom of the saucepan and begins to move away from the sides of the saucepan.

Place this flour-butter mixture in food processor and process until smooth. Add all remaining ingredients and process for another 20 seconds or so, until everything is well blended. Add reserved ground fish and continue processing until everything is thoroughly blended. You may have to do this in two or more steps.

Bring 2 to 3 inches of salted water to a slow simmer in a 12-inch skillet. Carefully slip tablespoonfuls of quenelle batter into simmering water and poach for 15 to 20 minutes un-covered. Do not allow water to boil. Quenelles are done when they have approximately doubled in size. Remove quenelles with a slotted spoon and place in a buttered casserole. Serve with hot Sauce aux Crevettes et Vin.

Serves: 8

Cuisinart processor: Steel knife blade

Other processors: Attachments manufacturer recommends for grinding and mixing

SAUCE AUX CREVETTES ET VIN

½ **pound shrimp, cooked, cleaned, and deveined, each shrimp cut in half**
3 tablespoons sweet butter
3 scallions, each one cut into 3 pieces
3 tablespoons flour
2 cups dry white wine
2 tablespoons tomato paste
½ **cup tomato sauce**
4 sprigs parsley
Salt and freshly ground black pepper to taste
1 cup heavy sweet cream

Place cooked shrimp in food processor and chop coarsely. Heat butter in a saucepan. Add scallions and flour and cook for 2 minutes, stirring. Add wine, tomato paste, tomato sauce, parsley, and salt and pepper. Bring to a simmer and cook for 30 minutes. Pour sauce into processor and process shrimp and sauce for about 20 seconds. Return contents of processor to saucepan and stir in cream. Bring to a simmer and cook for 3 to 5 minutes. Correct seasoning and serve over quenelles.

Cuisinart processor: Steel knife blade

Other processors: Blender or attachments manufacturer recommends for chopping and mixing

Oysters New Orleans

3 scallions, each cut into 3 pieces
1 stalk celery, cut into 3 pieces
2 stalks fresh fennel or finocchio, each stalk cut into 3 pieces
4 sprigs Italian parsley
4 tablespoons sweet butter
2 cups watercress
¼ pound sweet butter, cut into 6 or 8 pieces
½ cup homemade bread crumbs
½ cup anisette liqueur
Salt and freshly ground black pepper to taste
Few grains cayenne pepper
2 dozen absolutely fresh oysters, on the half-shell

Place scallions, celery, fennel, and parsley into food processor and chop coarsely. Melt 4 tablespoons of butter in a large skillet and add mixture from food processor. Sauté until vegetables are limp, about 3 to 5 minutes. Add watercress and cook, stirring, until watercress has wilted.

Return ingredients from skillet to processor and add ¼ pound butter, bread crumbs, and anisette. Process until mixture is thoroughly blended and smooth. Season to taste.

Place approximately 1 tablespoonful of mixture on top of each oyster and bake oysters in a preheated 450-degree oven until topping and oysters are hot, approximately 4 to 5 minutes.

Serves: 4

Cuisinart processor: Steel knife blade

Other processors: Blender or attachments manufacturer recommends for chopping and mixing

Cold Salmon Mousse

3 tablespoons lemon juice

2 tablespoons cold water

2 envelopes unflavored gelatin

⅔ cup boiling water

2 stalks celery, each one cut into 3 pieces

1 small onion, cut into 2 pieces

¼ medium cucumber, peeled and cut into 4 pieces

½ carrot, cut into 2 pieces

2 sprigs parsley

½ cup homemade mayonnaise

1 cup heavy sweet cream

¼ teaspoon white pepper

1 teaspoon salt

3 sprigs fresh dill

1 pound fresh salmon steaks, poached, with skin and bones removed, and cut into pieces (or 2 seven-and-three-quarter-ounce cans drained salmon)

Place lemon juice and cold water in food processor. Sprinkle gelatin on top and let stand 1 minute. Add boiling water and blend for about 10 seconds. Add remaining ingredients and process until mixture is thoroughly smooth. You may have to do this in two or more steps. Pour into a 5-cup fish-shaped mold. Chill overnight or for several hours, until firm. Serve on a bed of salad greens and garnish with lemon slices and pimientos.

Serves: 6

Cuisinart processor: Steel knife blade

Other processors: Blender or attachments manufacturer recommends for grinding and mixing

Salmon Steak with Lettuce Sauce

1 head, or more, iceberg lettuce
½ small onion
1 cup sour cream
2 tablespoons lime or lemon juice
1½ teaspoons salt
¼ teaspoon white pepper
1 cup milk
¼ pound sweet butter
1 medium potato, cubed, boiled, and drained
6 salmon steaks
Salt and pepper to taste
½ cup dry vermouth
6 lemon slices
6 tablespoons red caviar (salmon roe)
Ripe black olives

Core, rinse, and drain lettuce. Chop lettuce in food processor until you have 4 tightly packed cups of chopped lettuce. Remove and reserve. Chop onion in processor. Add sour cream, lime or lemon juice, salt and pepper and blend. Gradually add chopped lettuce until you have a smooth sauce. You may have to do this in two or more steps. When sauce is thoroughly blended, remove to a bowl.

Heat milk and 4 tablespoons butter in a saucepan. Place cooked potato cubes in processor. Add milk-butter mixture and puree potato. Allow mixture to cool, then blend gradually into previously prepared lettuce sauce. You may have to do this in two or more steps. Chill sauce.

Sprinkle salmon steaks with salt and pepper and place in a baking pan. Cut remaining butter into 6 pieces and place a piece of butter on each salmon steak. Pour vermouth over fish. Cover pan with foil and bake in a preheated 400-degree oven for about 20 minutes or until fish flakes easily with a fork.

Chill salmon steaks. Serve with a dollop of Lettuce Sauce on top and lemon slices. Garnish with red caviar and black olives.

Serves: 6

Cuisinart processor: Steel knife blade

Other processors: Blender or attachments manufacturer recommends for chopping, pureeing, and mixing

Sole Mousse and Cucumber Sauce

1¼ **pounds cooked filet of sole***
1 **cup milk**
1 **small onion**
2 **tablespoons flour**
6 **eggs**
3 **sprigs parsley**
½ **teaspoon salt**
3 **sprigs fresh dill**

Place fish in processor and grind until smooth. Add all other ingredients and continue processing until mixture is well-blended and smooth. You may have to do this in two or more steps. Pour mousse mixture into a well-greased 6-cup ring mold. Bake in a preheated 400-degree oven for about 50 to 60 minutes or until top is brown and puffy and knife inserted in center comes out clean. Remove from oven and serve warm with Cucumber Sauce.

* Cooked or canned salmon, tuna, or flounder, or cooked and cleaned shrimp may be substituted for the sole.

Serves: 8

Cuisinart processor: Steel knife blade

Other processors: Attachments manufacturer recommends for grinding and mixing

CUCUMBER SAUCE

½ cucumber, peeled and cut into 3 pieces
½ small onion
4 sprigs fresh dill
1 teaspoon salt
¼ teaspoon white pepper
2 cups sour cream

Place cucumber, onion, and dill in food processor and chop coarsely. Add salt, pepper, and sour cream and blend thoroughly. Spoon Cucumber Sauce into a bowl and serve with Sole Mousse.

Cuisinart processor: Steel knife blade

Other processors: Blender or attachments manufacturer recommends for chopping and mixing

))*)*

Tuna Shrimp Pie

1 single 9-inch baked pie crust shell (see page 198, All-American Pie Crust Dough)
1 seven-ounce can tuna, drained
½ pound shrimp, cooked, shelled, and deveined, each shrimp cut in half
½ cup pimiento-stuffed small green olives
½ cup heavy sweet cream
2 cups Béchamel sauce
Salt and freshly ground black pepper to taste
½ teaspoon mild paprika
Few grains cayenne pepper

Place baked pie shell in oven and keep warm, at approximately 200 degrees, until ready to use.

Place tuna and shrimp halves in food processor and process until ingredients are coarsely chopped and blended together. You may have to start and stop machine, pushing ingredients down from sides of the bowl.

Stir ¼ cup of olives into tuna-shrimp mixture, combining with a spoon. Reserve remainder of the olives for garnish. Place mixture in a large skillet or saucepan and add cream, Béchamel Sauce, and seasonings and bring to a simmer over a low heat, stirring from time to time.

Pour mixture into pie shell, garnish with remaining olives, and serve at once.

Serves: 6

Cuisinart processor: Steel knife blade

Other processors: Attachment manufacturer recommends for chopping or grinding

Béchamel Sauce

4 tablespoons butter
4 tablespoons flour
2 cups light sweet cream
Salt and freshly ground white pepper to taste
⅛ teaspoon nutmeg (optional)

Melt butter in a saucepan. Add flour and cook over low heat, stirring, for 3 to 5 minutes, making sure that flour does not burn. Bring cream to a simmer and add cream to butter-flour mixture. Whisk mixture, allowing it to come to a simmer, and cook, whisking or stirring for 3 to 5 minutes, until mixture thickens. Season to taste.

Yield: Approximately 2 cups

Tuna Timbale

2 cans (approximately 7 ounces) tuna, drained
½ cup homemade bread crumbs
4 tablespoons butter, cut into 4 pieces
2 eggs
3 sprigs parsley
3 tablespoons heavy sweet cream
Salt and freshly ground white pepper to taste
Dash of cayenne pepper

Place tuna in food processor and chop. Add other ingredients, one at a time, and continue processing until mixture is well blended. Spoon mixture into a buttered 4-cup mold or loaf pan. Place mold or pan into a larger pan of hot water and bake in a preheated 375-degree oven for 30 minutes.

Serves: 4 to 6

Cuisinart processor: Steel knife blade

Other processors: Attachments manufacturer recommends for chopping and mixing

VEGETABLES AND SALADS

Vegetables have been the object of bad publicity over the years. From childhood on, we are told how good vegetables are *for* us, but not how good they *are*. Nutrition rather than flavor is emphasized until vegetables soon have about as much appeal as medicine. Too often children grow up to despise vegetables, never really having had an opportunity to taste and appreciate them. With the advent of the food processor, the time has come to reverse all the anti-vegetable propaganda. Properly prepared, vegetables are delicious, nutritious, and beautiful. With the aid of a food processor you turn the most ordinary vegetables into delicately spiced and flavored purees, just like the vegetable purees served at the most expensive French restaurants. In addition, your processor will shred cabbage for cole slaw, puree avocado for perfect guacamole, and grate potatoes for potato pancakes—all in a matter of seconds.

Artichokes Stuffed with Ham and Mushrooms

4 large artichokes
¼ pound boiled ham, cut into cubes or strips
¼ pound mushrooms
1 small onion
½ cup olive oil
½ cup homemade bread crumbs
1 cup dry white wine
1 cup chicken broth

Cut off the stems of the artichokes and the tips of the leaves and remove tough outer leaves. Open up center of each artichoke, and using a spoon or a melon ball cutter, remove and discard choke from center of each artichoke. Wash artichokes well and reserve.

Chop ham, mushrooms, and onion in food processor. Heat olive oil in a large skillet and sauté ingredients from food processor for 10 to 15 minutes. Remove from heat and stir bread crumbs into mixture in skillet. Combine thoroughly. Stuff artichokes with mixture. Place artichokes in a baking dish, and pour wine and chicken broth over them. Cover dish with foil, and place in a preheated 350-degree oven for 1 hour or until artichokes are tender. Test by removing an artichoke leaf and tasting for tenderness.

Serves: 4

Cuisinart processor: Steel knife blade

Other processors: Attachment manufacturer recommends for chopping

ARTICHOKES STUFFED WITH HAM AND MUSHROOMS
Courtesy California Artichoke Advisory Board

Glazed Carrots

1½ pounds carrots, scraped
1 cup beef bouillon or 1 cup water
1 tablespoon sugar, or more, to taste
Salt and freshly ground black pepper to taste
¼ pound sweet butter

Slice the carrots in the food processor and then place sliced carrots in a saucepan. Add all other ingredients and cook until carrots are tender and the liquid has become a glaze. The length of cooking time will depend on the age of the carrots and can range anywhere from 15 to 40 minutes. Carrots should be firm to tender, and not mushy.

Serves: 4 to 6

Cuisinart processor: Slicing disc

Other processors: Attachment manufacturer recommends for slicing

A Bouquet of Cole Slaws

Cole slaws are a marvelous accompaniment to seafood, sandwiches, fried chicken, and barbecues. The food processor will slice or shred cabbage for a variety of slaws. Here are several recipes from which you can easily adapt your own favorites.

Cabbage and Bean Slaw

½ head of cabbage (about 1 pound), cored and cut into
   wedges
2 carrots
2 stalks celery
1 small onion
1 sixteen-ounce can red kidney beans, drained
½ teaspoon salt
1 cup mayonnaise, homemade
1 tablespoon wine vinegar
3 tablespoons olive oil

Slice cabbage, carrots, celery, and onion in food processor, doing this in as many steps as necessary until all vegetables are sliced. Place vegetables in a large bowl and add drained beans. Sprinkle salt on vegetables and toss with mayonnaise. Combine vinegar and olive oil and pour over slaw. Toss again until all ingredients are combined.

Serves: 4 to 6

Cuisinart processor: Slicing disc

Other processors: Attachments manufacturer recommends
   for shredding and slicing

Gingery Fruit Slaw

½ head of cabbage (about 1 pound), cored and cut into wedges
2 Bartlett pears, halved and cored
⅓ cup seedless grapes
1 cup homemade mayonnaise
3 teaspoons grated lemon rind
2 tablespoons lemon juice
2 teaspoons sugar
½ teaspoon ground ginger
¼ teaspoon salt

Slice or shred cabbage in food processor, doing this with slicing disc and in as many steps as necessary. Remove cabbage to a large salad bowl.

Using steel knife blade, coarsely chop pears in food processor. Remove to salad bowl and add whole grapes.

Blend remaining ingredients in food processor. Pour mixture over ingredients in bowl and toss. Chill 30 minutes before serving.

Serves: 4 to 6

Cuisinart processor: Slicing disc for cabbage; steel knife blade for chopping pears and blending dressing

Other Processors: Attachments manufacturer recommends for shredding or slicing, and chopping and blending

Hot Cole Slaw with Sherry Wine and Cheese

½ **head of cabbage (about 1 pound), cored and cut into wedges**

2 small onions

1 medium carrot, cut into 3 pieces

2 tablespoons butter

1 tablespoon sugar

½ **teaspoon salt**

¼ **cup dry sherry wine**

¼ **cup Parmesan cheese, grated**

Using slicing disc, slice or shred cabbage in food processor, doing this in as many steps as necessary until all cabbage is sliced. Slice onion in food processor. Remove cabbage and onion and reserve.

Changing to steel knife blade, grate carrot in food processor.

Melt butter in a large skillet and sauté all vegetables for 5 minutes. Add seasonings and sherry to skillet and continue cooking for 10 minutes, stirring from time to time. Place mixture in a baking dish, sprinkle with Parmesan cheese, and place in a preheated 425-degree oven until cheese melts, approximately 10 minutes.

Serves: 4 to 6

Cuisinart processor: Slicing disc for cabbage and onion; steel knife blade for grating carrot

Other processors: Attachments manufacturer recommends for slicing and grating

---

Old-Fashioned Cole Slaw

**1 small head of cabbage (about 1½ to 2 pounds), cored and
  cut into wedges**
2 carrots
1 green pepper, cored, seeded, and cut into 4 pieces
1 small onion
1 cup homemade mayonnaise
2 tablespoons vinegar
¼ cup milk
Salt and freshly ground black pepper to taste
2 teaspoons sugar

Using slicing disc, slice cabbage in food processor, doing this
in as many steps as necessary until all cabbage is sliced. Remove cabbage to a large bowl. Slice carrots and add to cabbage.

Changing to steel knife blade, chop green pepper and onion
in food processor; add to cabbage.

Blend all other ingredients in food processor and pour dressing
over vegetables. Toss to combine thoroughly, and serve.

Serves: 6 to 8

Cuisinart processor: Slicing disc for cabbage; steel knife
   blade for chopping green pepper and onion and for blending
   dressing

Other processors: Attachments manufacturer recommends
   for slicing or shredding, and for chopping and blending

Cabbage and Bow-Tie Noodles

½ head of cabbage (about 1 pound), cored and cut into
    wedges
Salt
1 large onion, cut into 4 pieces
1 cup cooking oil
2 tablespoons sugar, or more, to taste
Salt and freshly ground black pepper to taste
½ pound of bow-tie noodles, cooked al dente, or slightly
    firm

With slicing disc, slice or shred cabbage in food processor. Remove to a large bowl and salt liberally. Allow cabbage to stand for half an hour, and then, taking handfuls of cabbage, squeeze out excess water. Reserve cabbage.

Place onion in food processor and chop, using steel knife blade. Heat ¼ of oil in a large skillet and sauté onions until they are translucent. Add cabbage to skillet and sauté, stirring from time to time and adding more oil as necessary. Cover skillet and cook over a low heat for about 30 minutes or until cabbage is completely tender. Add sugar, salt, and lots of black pepper. Cabbage should have a sweet, spicy flavor. Cook an additional 5 minutes and then stir in cooked noodles. Correct seasoning and serve piping hot. This dish is especially good with roast duck or roast goose.

Serves: 8

Cuisinart processor: Slicing disc for cabbage; steel knife blade for onion

Other processors: Attachments manufacturer recommends for shredding or slicing, and chopping

Cucumber and Onion Salad

4 large cucumbers, peeled
2 large onions, peeled
Salt
3 cups water
4 tablespoons sugar, or more, to taste
1 cup white vinegar
Mild Hungarian paprika

Slice cucumbers and onions in food processor, removing as you slice to a large bowl. Sprinkle cucumbers and onions liberally with salt and stir. Allow vegetables to remain in salt for 20 minutes or until wilted. Squeeze water out of vegetables and return to bowl. (If you prefer a crisper salad, you may omit salting step.)

Combine all other ingredients and correct seasoning to taste. Pour water-vinegar mixture over cucumbers and onions and chill. Allow to stand at least 4 hours before serving.

This salad will be fine the next day, the day after, or as long as it lasts.

Serves: 8 to 10

Cuisinart processor: Slicing disc

Other processors: Attachment manufacturer recommends for slicing

Jellied Mousse of Cucumber

2 cucumbers, peeled and quartered
1 envelope unflavored gelatin
¼ cup cold water
2 tablespoons boiling water
1 tablespoon lemon juice
½ cup homemade mayonnaise
1 teaspoon salt
¼ teaspoon freshly ground white pepper
1 cup heavy whipping cream

Place cucumbers in food processor and puree.

Place gelatin in a small bowl and soften in cold water. Add hot water and stir. Add gelatin mixture and remaining ingredients to food processor and process until mixture is thoroughly smooth and blended.

Pour mixture into a 1-quart mold and chill overnight.

Serves: 8

Cuisinart processor: Steel knife blade

Other processors: Blender or attachments manufacturer recommends for pureeing and mixing

Fiesta Three-Bean Salad

1 green pepper, cored, seeded, and cut into 4 pieces
1 large onion
1 clove garlic
1 sixteen-ounce can chick-peas, drained
1 sixteen-ounce can red kidney beans, drained
1 sixteen-ounce can green cut beans, drained
2 tablespoons olive oil
5 tablespoons cider vinegar
¼ cup dark molasses
1½ teaspoons salt
Freshly ground black pepper to taste
1 teaspoon Worcestershire sauce
¼ teaspoon Tabasco
1½ teaspoons chili powder
½ teaspoon dry mustard

Chop green pepper, onion, and garlic clove in food processor. Remove to a large salad bowl. Add all beans to salad bowl. Place all other ingredients in food processor and blend thoroughly. Pour over salad ingredients and toss well. Chill two or more hours before serving, stirring occasionally.

Serves: 6

Cuisinart processor: Steel knife blade

Other processors: Blender or attachments manufacturer recommends for chopping and mixing

Guacamole Salad

2 large ripe avocados, peeled, pitted, and cut into chunks
1 clove garlic
1 small onion
2 teaspoons lemon juice
¼ teaspoon Tabasco, or a Mexican hot chili pepper, fresh or canned
1 tomato, cut in half
½ cup mayonnaise
Salt to taste

Place all ingredients, except mayonnaise, in food processor and chop coarsely. Add mayonnaise and salt and blend. Serve on lettuce, as a salad, or with corn chips or warm tortillas, as a dip.

Serves: 6

Cuisinart processor: Steel knife blade

Other processors: Attachment manufacturer recommends for chopping

Gallatin's Lettuce Soufflé

Gallatin's Restaurant, in Monterey, California, is deservedly proud of its varied menu, which features such items as Abalone Puffs, as well as more familiar continental dishes. The following Lettuce Soufflé is one of their more original dishes.

2 heads of iceberg lettuce, broken into large wedges
1 small onion
4 tablespoons sweet butter
3 tablespoons flour
1 cup milk, or half-and-half
1 teaspoon Worcestershire sauce
½ teaspoon salt
⅛ teaspoon pepper
4 eggs, separated
¼ pound Cheddar cheese
¼ teaspoon cream of tartar
Pinch of salt
2 tablespoons butter
1–2 tablespoons grated Parmesan cheese (optional)

Preheat oven to 400 degrees. Chop lettuce in food processor until you have 4 fully-packed cups of small lettuce pieces. (Be sure to use the dark, outer lettuce leaves as well as the heart of the lettuce.) Chop onion very finely in food processor.

Melt 1 tablespoon butter in a large saucepan and cook lettuce and onion, stirring, until both are tender. Remove vegetables with a slotted spoon and set aside.

Melt remaining 3 tablespoons butter in saucepan. Blend in flour, milk, Worcestershire sauce, salt, and pepper. Whisk, so there are no lumps, and cook, stirring, over medium heat until sauce thickens. This should take about 1 minute. Remove

GALLATIN'S LETTUCE SOUFFLÉ
Courtesy Western Iceberg Lettuce, Inc.

sauce from heat and beat in egg yolks, one at a time. Cube Cheddar cheese, place in processor, and grate. Blend grated cheese into sauce and stir in lettuce-onion combination.

Place egg whites, cream of tartar, and salt in food processor and whip until stiff but not dry. Fold egg whites into lettuce mixture.

Butter bottom and sides of a 6-cup soufflé baking dish and sprinkle with Parmesan cheese, if desired. Spoon lettuce mixture into soufflé dish and smooth top. Again, sprinkle with Parmesan cheese, if desired. Place soufflé in middle of oven. Reduce heat to 375 degrees. Bake 25 to 30 minutes, but do not open oven door for at least 20 minutes. Soufflé should be puffed and lightly browned on top.

Serves: 4

Cuisinart processor: Steel knife blade for chopping lettuce and onion, grating cheese, and beating egg whites

Other processors: Attachments manufacturer recommends for chopping, grating, and beating

Gallatin's Spiced Stuffed Tomatoes

LETTUCE FILLING FOR BAKED TOMATOES

2 heads iceberg lettuce, broken into large wedges
2 scallions, cut into 2 pieces each
3 tablespoons sweet butter
Pinch of cayenne pepper
Pinch of nutmeg
Salt to taste

Chop lettuce and scallions in food processor. You should have 8 cups of tightly-packed shredded lettuce. Steam lettuce and scallions in very little water until tender. Drain and cool. Puree lettuce mixture in food processor.

Melt butter in a saucepan. Add lettuce and remaining ingredients. Cook, stirring, until most of the liquid is evaporated, about 10 minutes. Use as a filling for Baked Tomatoes.

Cuisinart processor: Steel knife blade

Other processors: Attachments manufacturer recommends for chopping and pureeing

BAKED TOMATOES

6 ripe medium tomatoes
¼ pound Gruyère cheese, cut into cubes
¼ cup sugar
¼ cup butter
Pinch of salt

Cut tops from tomatoes and scoop out insides. Place tomato pulp in food processor and chop. Reserve. Spoon Spiced Lettuce mixture into tomato cases. Place Gruyère cheese cubes in food processor and chop; sprinkle filled tomatoes with the cheese.

Place tomato pulp in a saucepan and add sugar, butter, and salt. Cook tomato mixture until it is soft and well blended.

Pour tomato mixture into a buttered baking dish. Arrange stuffed tomatoes on top, and bake in a preheated 400-degree oven for 15 minutes.

Serves: 6

Cuisinart processor: Steel knife blade

Other processors: Attachments manufacturer recommends for chopping or pureeing

Green Beans and Almond Puree

1½ pounds of green beans, cooked until tender and drained
1 cup chicken broth, homemade or canned
¼ pound sweet butter
½ cup sour cream
Salt and freshly ground black pepper to taste
¼ cup slivered almonds

Place green beans in food processor and process until completely pureed. You may have to do this in two or more steps. Add chicken broth and continue processing until thoroughly blended.

Melt butter in a skillet and spoon mixture from processor into skillet. Cook, stirring, over low heat, until puree begins to simmer; then stir in sour cream and season to taste. Continue cooking until puree is thoroughly hot. Serve with slivered almonds as a garnish.

Serves: 6

Cuisinart processor: Steel knife blade

Other processors: Attachments manufacturer recommends for pureeing and mixing

Potato and Celery Root Puree

4 large potatoes, peeled, cubed, boiled, and drained
2 large celery roots (celery knob), peeled, cubed, boiled, and
  drained
1 cup chicken broth, homemade or canned
Salt and freshly ground black pepper to taste
¼ pound sweet butter
½ cup, or more, heavy sweet cream

Place potatoes and celery roots in food processor and puree, gradually adding all other ingredients. This may have to be done in two or more steps. Correct seasoning.

Serves: 6 to 8

Cuisinart processor: Steel knife blade

Other processors: Attachments manufacturer recommends for pureeing and mixing

Doubly Delicious Baked Potatoes with Caviar

We are indebted to Mr. Craig Claiborne, who inspired this recipe. Indeed, a whole world of people who like delicious food are indebted to Mr. Claiborne, for this and other fine cooking inventions.

8 Idaho baking potatoes
¼ pound, or more, sweet butter
3 scallions, each one cut into 3 pieces
1 cup milk
½ cup heavy sweet cream
½ cup sour cream
Salt and freshly ground white pepper
8 ounces black caviar, or whitefish roe

In a preheated oven of 350 degrees, bake potatoes for 1 hour or until tender. Remove potatoes from oven and slice off tops lengthwise. Scoop potato pulp from shell into food processor, and puree potatoes in two or more steps. Gradually add all other ingredients except caviar. Continue processing until mixture is thoroughly blended and pureed. Turn machine on and off as you process, scraping mixture down from sides of bowl. Add more butter, milk, or cream if you wish. Spoon potato puree back into bottom half of potato shells and place these stuffed potatoes in a baking dish. Before serving, place in preheated 400-degree oven and heat thoroughly. Remove hot potatoes from oven and garnish each potato with a tablespoonful of caviar.

Serves: 8

Cuisinart processor: Steel knife blade

Other processors: Attachment manufacturer recommends for pureeing

Jerry's Potato Chips

2 pounds potatoes, peeled
½ cup, or more, cooking oil
Salt

Heat ¼ cup oil in a large skillet.*

Slice potatoes thinly in food processor. Rinse potatoes in cold water and dry thoroughly on paper towels.

When oil is hot and bubbling slightly, slip potato slices into skillet, a few slices at a time. Fry potatoes in batches until potatoes are crisp and golden brown. Add more oil as necessary.

Drain potatoes on paper towels, sprinkle with salt, and keep warm in a 250-degree oven until all chips are fried and you are ready to serve them.

* Potatoes may also be cooked in a deep-fat fryer. Heat oil to a temperature of 375 to 400 degrees. Fill basket of deep-fat fryer with potatoes. Dip in and out of hot oil until bubbling occurs. Continue in-and-out motion until bubbling stops.

When bubbling stops, allow potatoes to remain in basket, immersed in oil, until potatoes are golden brown. Drain potatoes on paper towels, salt, and serve at once.

Serves: 6

Cuisinart processor: Slicing disc

Other processors: Attachment manufacturer recommends for slicing

Mother's Potato Pancakes

4 potatoes, peeled
1 small onion
1 egg
2 tablespoons flour
Salt and freshly ground black pepper to taste
Butter or oil for frying

Place potatoes in food processor equipped with shredding disc, and shred or grate. Shred or grate onion. Add egg, flour, and seasonings to potato mixture in food processor, and using plastic mixing blade or steel knife blade, blend thoroughly. Remove mixture to a bowl.

Heat butter or oil in a large skillet and drop tablespoonfuls of batter into skillet. Press back of spoon down on each pancake to make it thin. Fry on both sides until crispy and brown. Serve at once.

Serves: 3 to 4

Cuisinart processor: Shredding disc for potatoes and onion; plastic mixing blade or steel knife blade for blending

Other processors: Attachments manufacturer recommends for shredding or grating, and blending or mixing

Potato Cheese Casserole

1½ pounds potatoes, peeled, cubed, boiled, and drained
1 three-ounce package cream cheese
¼ pound Cheddar cheese, cut into cubes
1 cup creamed cottage cheese
2 tablespoons butter
¼ cup milk
2 teaspoons dried chives
3 sprigs parsley
½ teaspoon white pepper
Mild paprika

Place potatoes in food processor and puree until smooth. Add remaining ingredients, except paprika, and continue processing until smooth. You may have to do this in two or more steps. Spoon potato mixture into a buttered 1-quart baking dish. Sprinkle top with paprika. Bake in a preheated 350-degree oven for 30 to 40 minutes or until piping hot.

Serves: 6

Cuisinart processor: Steel knife blade

Other processors: Blender or attachment manufacturer recommends for pureeing

Sweet Potato Pudding

4 baked sweet potatoes
1 cup brown sugar
½ cup melted butter
4 egg yolks
2 teaspoons grated lemon rind
1 cup orange juice
4 egg whites
½ teaspoon cream of tartar

Scoop sweet potato pulp out of shells into food processor fitted with steel knife blade. Gradually add all ingredients, except egg whites and cream of tartar, and puree until all ingredients are thoroughly blended. Spoon mixture into a buttered baking or soufflé dish.

Wash and dry work bowl of food processor thoroughly. Changing to plastic mixing blade, place egg whites in processor, add cream of tartar, and beat until thick. Fold egg whites into sweet potato mixture and place baking dish in a preheated 350-degree oven for 1 hour.

Serves: 4 to 6

Cuisinart processor: Steel knife blade for potatoes; plastic mixing blade for egg whites

Other processors: Attachments manufacturer recommends for pureeing, and beating or whipping

White Bean and Chestnut Puree

3 cups cooked and drained white beans (may be canned)
1 cup canned unsweetened chestnut puree
Salt and freshly ground black pepper to taste
¼ pound sweet butter
½ cup heavy sweet cream
1 teaspoon sugar, or more, to taste

Place beans in food processor and puree until completely smooth. You may have to do this in two or more steps. Add chestnuts to processor and continue processing until completely blended. Season. Melt butter in a saucepan and add bean-chestnut mixture. Cook, stirring, for 2 to 3 minutes and then stir in cream, gradually. Add sugar to taste and continue stirring over low heat until puree is thoroughly warm. This puree is especially delicious with roast lamb.

Serves: 6 to 8

Cuisinart processor: Steel knife blade

Other processors: Attachment manufacturer recommends for pureeing

South-of-the-Border Salad

1 head iceberg lettuce
⅓ cup olive oil
2 tablespoons wine vinegar
1 clove garlic
Salt and freshly ground black pepper to taste
1 fifteen-ounce can garbanzos, or chick-peas, drained
3 stalks celery, each stalk cut into 3 pieces
4 scallions, each scallion cut into 3 pieces
½ cup croutons, sautéed in oil until crisp

Core, rinse, and drain lettuce. Shred lettuce in food processor and remove to a salad bowl. Now using steel knife blade, blend oil, wine vinegar, and garlic in food processor. Remove dressing and reserve. Add garbanzos to lettuce in salad bowl. Place celery and scallions in food processor and chop coarsely. Add to salad bowl. Toss with dressing and garnish with croutons. Serve at once.

Serves: 6

Cuisinart processor: Shredding disc for lettuce; steel knife blade for blending dressing with garlic and chopping celery and scallions

Other processors: Attachments manufacturer recommends for shredding, blending, and chopping

Creamy Spinach Puree

2 pounds fresh cooked spinach
¼ pound sweet butter
1 tablespoon flour
Salt and freshly ground black pepper to taste
Pinch of nutmeg
1 cup, or more, heavy sweet cream

Puree spinach in food processor. Melt butter in a large sauce-pan and spoon spinach into hot butter. Cook, stirring, for 3 minutes. Stir in flour and continue cooking, stirring, for another 3 to 5 minutes. Add seasonings and stir in cream gradually. Bring to a simmer and cook over low heat for 5 to 10 minutes. Correct seasoning and add more cream if you wish.

Serves: 4 to 6

Cuisinart processor: Steel knife blade

Other processors: Attachment manufacturer recommends for pureeing

STEAMED PEAS WITH LETTUCE AND ONIONS
Courtesy Western Iceberg Lettuce, Inc.

Steamed Peas with Lettuce and Onions

1 medium head iceberg lettuce
2 cups water
Salt
1 pound small white boiling onions
1 ten-ounce package frozen green peas
4 tablespoons melted sweet butter
⅛ teaspoon nutmeg
½ teaspoon dried tarragon, crumbled

Core, rinse, and drain lettuce. Cut lettuce into wedges. Shred lettuce in food processor and reserve. Heat water, with 1 teaspoon salt, to boiling in a 2½-quart saucepan. Add onions and cook covered 10 to 15 minutes or until onions are almost tender.

Place vegetable steamer basket in saucepan over onions. Add peas to basket and sprinkle with salt. Cover and steam 8 minutes. Uncover and add shredded lettuce to steamer basket and steam 2 to 3 minutes or until thoroughly heated.

Place lettuce in center of serving dish and arrange peas and drained onions on lettuce. Add nutmeg and tarragon to melted butter and drizzle over peas.

Serves: 4 to 6

Cuisinart processor: Shredding disc

Other processors: Attachment manufacturer recommends for shredding

Zucchini in Sour Cream and Dill Sauce

8 medium zucchini, peeled
1 small onion
8 sprigs fresh dill
¼ pound sweet butter
Salt and freshly ground white pepper to taste
Juice of one lemon
2 tablespoons sugar, or more, to taste
2 teaspoons flour
2 cups sour cream
½ teaspoon mild paprika

Slice zucchini in food processor, remove, and reserve. Next, chop onion and dill in food processor. Melt butter in a saucepan and add zucchini, onion, and dill to hot butter. Season with salt and white pepper. Cover saucepan and cook over medium heat until zucchini is firm to tender, and not mushy. This can take approximately 15 to 20 minutes. Sprinkle lemon over zucchini, add sugar, and cook for another 2 minutes, stirring. Stir flour into sour cream until well blended. Gradually add sour cream mixture to zucchini, stirring. Stir in paprika. Cook, over a low heat, until sauce thickens slightly, about another 5 to 10 minutes.

Serves: 6 to 8

Cuisinart processor: Slicing disc for zucchini; steel knife blade for chopping onion and dill

Other processors: Attachments manufacturer recommends for slicing and chopping

BREADS, PASTRIES, AND PASTAS

The difficulty of preparing your own breads, pastries, and pasta dough is now a thing of the past. You no longer have to worry about not having a fine hand for working pie crusts or tart shells. Your food processor will do the initial mixing and kneading for you. If you are working with the Cuisinart processor, remember it has a smaller capacity and can make only one loaf of bread at a time. However, the machine works so quickly that it won't take you more than a few minutes to prepare a second batch of pie crust, tart, or bread dough.

Machines equipped with dough hooks can prepare larger batches of dough at one time, and with that in mind we have included in this chapter a special collection of bread recipes for food processors with dough hooks.

Brioche

1 quarter-ounce package active dry yeast
2 tablespoons warm milk (105 to 115 degrees)
2 tablespoons all-purpose flour
⅓ cup sweet butter, cut into chunks
2 tablespoons plus 2 teaspoons sugar
¼ teaspoon salt
1 egg
1¼–1½ cups all-purpose flour
1 egg beaten with one tablespoonful milk

In a small bowl, sprinkle yeast over warm milk. Allow it to soften for 2 to 3 minutes, and then stir in 2 tablespoons flour. Cover and let rise in a warm place until doubled, about 1 hour.

Place butter, sugar, and salt in food processor and cut butter into sugar. Process until smooth, about 30 seconds. Turn the machine on and off, leaving the machine on for about 10 seconds each time. (Turning the machine on and off is advisable when cutting shortening into sugar or flour for a more even blend.) Add yeast starter mixture, egg, and flour, ½ cup at a time. Blend with the same on/off action for about 20 seconds or until flour is blended in. Remove dough to a floured board and knead for 5 minutes.

Place dough in a large greased mixing bowl. Cover and allow to rise in a warm, draft-free place for 2½ hours or until more than doubled. Shape three-fourths of the dough into eight 2-inch balls. Place in greased brioche tins or muffin pans. Form remaining dough into 8 small ovals, about ½ to ¾ inch in diameter. Make a depression in the center of each large ball and fit small ovals into depression.

Cover and allow brioche to rise in a warm, draft-free place for about 1 hour, until dough has risen to top of each pan. Brush tops with egg-milk mixture. Bake in a preheated 400-degree oven for 12 to 15 minutes or until golden brown.

Yield: 8

Cuisinart processor: Steel knife blade

Other processors: Dough hook or other attachment manufacturer recommends for kneading

---

Banana Bread

¼ **pound butter, cut into 6 or 8 pieces**
1 **cup sugar**
2 **eggs**
4 **very ripe bananas, peeled, each one cut into 3 pieces**
2 **cups all-purpose flour**
1 **teaspoon baking powder**
1 **teaspoon baking soda**
¼ **teaspoon salt**

Place butter, sugar, and eggs in food processor. Process until all ingredients are blended. Add bananas and process again until bananas are blended into mixture.

Combine flour, baking powder, baking soda, and salt and add gradually to food processor. Turn the machine on and off while processing and push mixture down from sides of the bowl. Process until flour disappears into other ingredients.

Spoon mixture into a greased 9×5×3-inch loaf pan. Bake in a preheated 350-degree oven for 1 hour.

Yield: 1 loaf

Cuisinart processor: Steel knife blade

Other processors: Dough hook or attachment manufacturer recommends for kneading or mixing

Orange Marmalade Nut Bread

½ cup orange marmalade
1 egg yolk
½ cup milk
1 tablespoon grated orange peel
½ cup shelled pecans
1 teaspoon salt
2 cups all-purpose flour
2 teaspoons baking powder

Place marmalade, egg yolk, milk, orange peel, pecans, and salt in food processor. Process until ingredients are blended. Combine flour and baking powder and add gradually to food processor. Turn the machine on and off while processing and push mixture down from sides of the bowl. Process until flour disappears into other ingredients.

Spoon mixture into a buttered 9×5×3-inch loaf pan. Allow mixture to rest for 20 minutes. Bake in a preheated 350-degree oven for 45 minutes.

Yield: 1 loaf

Cuisinart processor: Steel knife blade

Other processors: Dough hook or attachment manufacturer recommends for kneading or mixing

Special Recipes for Machines Equipped with Dough Hooks

The following recipes were developed for machines that come equipped with dough hooks:

Apricot Pecan Coffee Ring, Brioche, Cheddar Cheese Bread, Easy Sour Cream Rolls, Oatmeal Raisin Bread, Pizza, Rye Bread, Swedish Tea Ring, Whole Wheat Bread, Honey White Bread

Apricot Pecan Coffee Ring

1¼ **cups milk**
½ **cup sugar**
½ **cup butter**
1 **teaspoon salt**
2 **quarter-ounce packages active dry yeast**
5–6 **cups all-purpose flour**
3 **eggs**
1 **egg, beaten with 1 tablespoon milk**

FILLING:

1½ **cups apricot preserves and**
   1 **cup chopped pecans, mixed together**

In a small saucepan, heat milk, sugar, and butter to 115 degrees. Butter does not have to be completely melted.

In large mixer bowl fitted with dough hook, combine salt, yeast, 5 cups of flour, and 3 eggs. Add the remaining cup of flour during kneading, if necessary.

Add milk mixture to ingredients in mixer bowl and mix at a low speed for about 3 minutes or until combined. Knead at a low to medium speed for 10 minutes or until dough is smooth and elastic.

Place dough in a well-greased bowl, cover, and allow to rise in a warm, draft-free place for 1½ hours or until dough has doubled in bulk.

Divide dough in half. Roll each half into an 18-inch by 12-inch rectangle. Place half of filling mixture in the center of each rectangle, spreading filling down the length of each strip to within 1 inch of ends. Roll each rectangle of dough tightly, jelly-roll style, starting with the long side. Seal well.

Form each rectangle of rolled dough into a ring and make slits in the dough 2 inches apart and 1 inch deep. Press to flatten.

Place rings on a cookie sheet, cover, and allow to rise in a warm, draft-free place for about 1 hour or until dough has doubled in bulk. Brush with egg-milk mixture.

Bake in a preheated 375-degree oven for 35 minutes or until well browned. Serve warm, or allow cake to cool, and sprinkle with powdered or confectioner's sugar.

Yield: 2 coffee cakes

For food processors equipped with dough hooks

Brioche

2 quarter-ounce packages active dry yeast
⅓ cup warm milk (105 to 115 degrees)
½ cup all-purpose flour
4–5 cups all-purpose flour
¼ cup sugar
1 teaspoon salt
5 eggs, beaten
1 egg beaten with 1 tablespoon milk

In a small bowl, sprinkle yeast over milk, allow to soften for 2 to 3 minutes, and then stir in ½ cup of flour. Cover and let rise in a warm, draft-free place for about 1 hour or until doubled in bulk.

In large mixer bowl, combine remaining ingredients. Start with 4 cups of flour and add remaining cup during kneading, if necessary.

Add yeast mixture to bowl and mix at low speed with dough hook for about 3 minutes or until combined. Knead with dough hook at low to medium speed for about 8 minutes or until dough is smooth and elastic.

Place dough in a well-greased bowl, cover, and allow to rise in a warm, draft-free place for 2 to 2½ hours or until doubled in bulk.

Shape three quarters of the dough into 24 two-inch balls. Place in greased brioche tins or muffin tins. Form remaining dough into 24 small ovals about ½ to ¾ inch in diameter.

Make a depression in the center of each large ball. Fit small ovals into depression.

Cover and allow brioche to rise in a warm, draft-free place for about 1 hour or until dough has risen to the top of each tin. Brush top of each brioche with egg-milk mixture.

Bake in preheated 400-degree oven for 12 to 15 minutes or until golden brown.

Yield: 24 brioches

For food processors equipped with dough hooks

Cheddar Cheese Bread

2¼ cups water
¼ cup butter
1 cup grated Cheddar cheese
2 tablespoons grated Parmesan cheese
2 tablespoons chives
¾ cup nonfat dry milk solids
2 quarter-ounce packages active dry yeast
5½–6½ cups all-purpose flour
¼ cup melted butter
Poppy seeds or sesame seeds

In a small saucepan, heat water and butter to 115 degrees. This butter does not have to be completely melted. In large mixer bowl fitted with dough hook, combine Cheddar cheese, Parmesan cheese, chives, dry milk, yeast, and 5½ cups flour. Add the remaining cup of flour during kneading, if necessary. Add water-butter mixture to bowl and mix at a low speed for about 3 minutes or until combined.

Knead at low to medium speed for about 10 minutes or until dough is smooth and elastic. Dough will be soft. Divide dough in half. Roll dough out on a floured board into two 14×7-inch rectangles.

Roll each rectangle tightly, jelly-roll style, beginning with the small side. Seal edges, and tuck in ends. Place seam side down in two well-greased 9×5×3-inch pans. Brush tops of loaves with melted butter and sprinkle with poppy seeds or sesame seeds.

Cover and let rise in a warm, draft-free place for 1½ hours or until doubled in bulk. Bake in a preheated 375-degree oven for 45 minutes or until well browned.

Yield: 2 loaves

For food processors equipped with dough hooks

Easy Sour Cream Rolls

1¼ cups water
¼ cup butter
¾ cup sour cream
1 teaspoon salt
2 teaspoons dill weed
1 tablespoon grated Parmesan cheese
⅓ cup nonfat dry milk solids
2 quarter-ounce packages active dry yeast
4–5½ cups all-purpose flour
½ cup melted butter

In a small saucepan, heat water and ¼ cup butter to 115 degrees. (This butter does not have to be completely melted.) In a large mixer bowl fitted with dough hook, combine next 7 ingredients.

Start by working in 4½ cups of flour and add the remaining cup during kneading, if necessary.

Add warm water-butter mixture to ingredients in bowl and mix with dough hook at a low speed for about 3 minutes or until combined. Knead at low to medium speed for about 7 to 10 minutes or until dough is smooth and elastic.

Form dough into 2-inch balls and place in greased muffin tins. Cover and let rise in a warm, draft-free place for about 1½ hours or until dough has about doubled in bulk. Brush tops with melted butter and bake in a preheated 375-degree oven for 30 minutes or until rolls are well browned.

Yield: 24 rolls

For food processors equipped with dough hooks

Oatmeal Raisin Bread

2 cups oatmeal
½ cup dark molasses
½ cup orange juice
½ cup raisins
⅓ cup vegetable oil
1 tablespoon salt
2 cups boiling water
1 quarter-ounce package active dry yeast
½ cup warm water (105 to 115 degrees)
6–6½ cups all-purpose flour
1 egg, beaten with 1 tablespoon milk

In large mixer bowl fitted with dough hook, combine oatmeal, molasses, orange juice, raisins, vegetable oil, salt, and boiling water. Mix well to combine. Allow oats to soften for half an hour.

When oats have softened, sprinkle yeast on warm water and allow to stand for 2 to 3 minutes. Stir to dissolve.

Add yeast mixture to oatmeal mixture in large mixer bowl. Add 2 cups of flour and begin blending at a low speed with dough hook.

Add remaining flour, ½ cup at a time, until mixture is well combined. Use higher speed to blend, if necessary. When all flour has been added, knead for about 10 minutes with dough hook.

Place dough in a greased bowl. Cover and let rise in a warm, draft-free place for about 1½ to 2 hours or until dough has doubled in bulk. Punch dough down and form into a ball. Cover and allow to rise again for about 1 hour.

Place dough on a floured board. Divide dough into 3 portions and form into round or oval loaves. Cover and let rise again until dough has risen by half, about 1½ hours. Brush tops of loaves with egg-milk mixture. Bake in a preheated 350-degree oven for 35 to 40 minutes or until golden brown.

Yield: 3 loaves

For food processors equipped with dough hooks

Pizza

2 quarter-ounce packages active dry yeast
1¼ cups warm water (105 to 115 degrees)
3¼ cups all-purpose flour
Pinch of sugar
1 teaspoon salt
¼ teaspoon pepper
½ teaspoon dry basil
2 cups tomato sauce, homemade or canned
½ pound mozzarella cheese, grated
3 tablespoons grated Parmesan cheese
2 teaspoons dry oregano
½ teaspoon garlic salt
Sliced green peppers, sautéed sliced onion, sliced mush-
rooms, sliced anchovies, to taste

In large mixer bowl, sprinkle yeast over ¼ cup warm water. Allow to stand about 2 minutes to dissolve. Stir. Add 1½ cups flour, sugar, salt, pepper, and basil to bowl. Mix at low speed with dough hook until all ingredients are combined.

Add remaining flour, ½ cup at a time, until all the flour has been added. Knead with dough hook for about 5 minutes or until dough is elastic and shiny.

Place dough in a floured bowl. Cover and allow to rise in a warm, draft-free place for 2 to 3 hours or until dough has doubled in bulk. Stretch dough to fit one 13×19×1½-inch pan or two 12-inch round pans.

Cover pizza dough with tomato sauce and cheese, and sprinkle with oregano and garlic salt. Add any combination of remaining ingredients listed.

Bake pizza in preheated 450-degree oven for 20 minutes or until crust is brown, sauce hot, and cheese melted.

Serves: 8 to 10

For food processors equipped with dough hooks

❋ʃ❋ʃ❋ʃ❋

Rye Bread

2 cups rye flour
¼ cup dark molasses
⅓ cup vegetable oil
2 teaspoons salt
2 cups boiling water
1 quarter-ounce package active dry yeast
½ cup warm water (105 to 115 degrees)
2 teaspoons caraway seeds
6–6½ cups all-purpose flour
1 egg beaten with 1 tablespoon milk

In large mixer bowl, combine rye flour, molasses, vegetable oil, salt, and boiling water. Stir well to combine, and cool to lukewarm, 105 to 115 degrees.

Sprinkle yeast over ½ cup of warm water and allow to soften for 2 to 3 minutes. Add to mixture in bowl. Add caraway seeds and 2 cups of flour and begin blending, using dough hook, at low speed. Add remaining flour, ½ cup at a time, until combined.

Knead with dough hook at low to medium speed for about 8 minutes or until dough is smooth and elastic. Place in a well-greased bowl, cover, and let rise in a warm, draft-free place for about 1½ to 2 hours or until doubled in bulk.

Punch dough down and form into a ball. Cover and allow to rise again for 1 hour.

Place dough on floured board and divide into 3 equal portions. Form into balls or oval loaves. Cover and allow to rise again in a warm, draft-free place for about 1½ hours or until dough has risen by half.

Brush tops of loaves with egg-milk mixture and bake in a preheated 350-degree oven for 35 to 40 minutes or until well browned.

Yield: 3 loaves

For food processors equipped with dough hooks

Swedish Tea Ring

¼ cup warm water (105 to 115 degrees)
1 quarter-ounce package active dry yeast
¾ cup warm milk (105 to 115 degrees)
¼ cup melted butter
1 egg
3–3¾ cups all-purpose flour
1 teaspoon salt
¼ cup sugar

FILLING:

½ cup sugar
2 teaspoons cinnamon
½ cup melted butter
½ cup raisins
¼ cup maraschino cherries, coarsely chopped
¼ cup walnuts, coarsely chopped

Dissolve yeast in warm water in mixer bowl. Allow to stand about 2 minutes. Add milk, butter, and egg to yeast mixture and mix, using dough hook, on low speed until combined.

Add 1 cup of flour, salt, and sugar and mix with dough hook at medium speed. Gradually add remaining flour and blend at low speed until dough forms a ball, about 8 to 10 minutes.

Remove dough and place in a well-greased bowl. Cover and set in a warm, draft-free place for 1½ hours. Punch down, cover, and let rise again for 30 minutes. Punch down.

On a floured board, roll dough into a rectangle 14 inches long and 10 inches wide. Combine sugar and cinnamon. Brush

SWEDISH TEA RING
Courtesy Sunbeam Mixmaster

top of rectangle with melted butter and sprinkle sugar-cinnamon mixture over dough.

Distribute raisins, cherries, and nuts over dough. Roll dough up tightly from wide end. Seal seam securely. Form a ring and seal ends together. Cut ⅔ of the way through the ring at 1-inch intervals. Twist sections on side.

Let dough rise for 20 to 30 minutes. Bake in a preheated 325-degree oven for 30 to 40 minutes or until top is golden brown.

If you should wish to glaze this tea ring, combine ½ cup powdered sugar with 1 tablespoonful of warm water and drizzle over cooled tea ring.

Yield: 1 Tea Ring

For food processors equipped with dough hooks

Whole Wheat Braid Bread

1 quarter-ounce package active dry yeast
1¼ cups warm water (105 to 115 degrees)
¼ pound butter, cut into 6 pieces
¼ cup honey
2 eggs
2 teaspoons salt
⅓ cup nonfat dry milk solids
4 cups all-purpose flour
2 cups whole wheat flour
1 egg beaten with 1 tablespoon milk
Sesame seeds or poppy seeds

In large mixer bowl, sprinkle yeast over warm water, allowing it to soften for 2 to 3 minutes. Stir to dissolve. Add butter, honey, eggs, salt, and nonfat dry milk solids to mixing bowl.

Using dough hook, blend for about 1 minute at low speed. Add flour, 1 cup at a time, mixing at low speed until well combined. Knead with dough hook for 8 to 10 minutes, or until dough is elastic and shiny. Dough will be soft.

Place dough in a lightly greased bowl. Cover and allow to rise in a warm, draft-free place for about 2 hours or until dough has doubled in bulk.

On a board, divide risen dough into 6 equal pieces. Allow dough to rest for about 10 minutes. Roll each piece into an 18-inch by 1-inch strand. Lay three strands of dough side by side on the board and start to braid the dough from the center to the bottom and then to the top. Tuck ends under.

Place each braided loaf on a baking sheet. Cover and allow to rise in a warm place for 1 hour or until size has increased by half.

Before baking, brush the top of each loaf with egg-milk combination. Sprinkle with sesame seeds or poppy seeds. Bake in a preheated 375-degree oven for 45 minutes or until loaves are well browned.

Yield: 2 large loaves

For food processors equipped with dough hooks

Honey White Bread

1 cup warm water (105 to 115 degrees)
2 quarter-ounce packages active dry yeast
1½ cups warm milk (105 to 115 degrees)
2 tablespoons honey
2 teaspoons salt
⅓ cup vegetable oil
6–7 cups all-purpose flour

In large mixer bowl, sprinkle yeast over warm water and allow it to stand 2 to 3 minutes to soften. Stir to dissolve. Add milk, honey, salt, oil, and 3 cups flour.

Using dough hook, blend at low speed until all flour is incorporated. Add remaining flour, ½ cup at a time. Amount of flour to be added will vary due to porosity of flour. Add only enough flour to form a ball.

Knead with dough hook for 5 minutes or until dough is shiny and elastic. Shape dough into 2 balls. Allow to rest for 10 minutes. Roll each ball of dough into an oval. Fold each oval in half, lengthwise. Pinch the seams to seal, and tuck the ends under. Place seam side down in 2 well-greased 9×5×3-inch pans.

Cover and let rise in a warm, draft-free place for 1 to 1½ hours or until doubled in bulk. Bake in a preheated 350-degree oven for approximately 45 minutes or until well browned.

Yield: 2 loaves

For food processors equipped with dough hooks

Spicy Raisin Tea Loaf

¼ **cup (or 1 stick) butter, cut into 6 or 8 pieces**
½ **cup sugar**
½ **cup light or dark molasses**
2 eggs
⅔ **cup milk**
1 carrot, peeled and cut into 6 pieces
1 cup walnuts
½ **cup dark raisins**
1 teaspoon vanilla extract
1 cup all-purpose flour
1½ **cups whole wheat flour**
3 teaspoons baking powder
½ **teaspoon each, cinnamon, nutmeg, and allspice**

Place butter, sugar, molasses, eggs, milk, carrot, walnuts, raisins, and vanilla into food processor. Process until ingredients are blended. Add flour, baking powder, and spices gradually to food processor. Turn the machine on and off while processing and process only as long as it takes flour to disappear into other ingredients.

Spoon dough into a greased and floured 9×5×3-inch loaf pan. Bake in a preheated 350-degree oven for 1 hour or until loaf feels firm to the touch. Remove from pan and allow to cool. Serve in thin slices with butter, cream cheese, jam, or marmalade.

Yield: 1 loaf

Cuisinart processor: Steel knife blade

Other processors: Dough hook or attachment manufacturer recommends for kneading

Pâte Brisée for Pies, Tarts, and Quiches

There are a variety of fine recipes for pâte brisée, *or French pastry dough. We offer a few recipes here, and with a bit of experimentation, you will soon find your favorite. When working with* pâte brisée, *remember the following:*

Flour varies in porosity, and you may find it necessary to adjust the recipe for less or more flour to create a dough with the proper consistency and texture.

If pastry dough does not form a ball as you're processing, add a bit more liquid. Be sure, however, to add the water in very small amounts.

Refrigerated pâte brisée *dough is easier to work with, and we suggest you chill dough for at least 30 minutes before using.*

Pâte brisée *dough can be stored in the refrigerator for approximately two days and kept in the freezer for months.*

Pâte Brisée I

> 1⅓ cups all-purpose flour
> ¼ pound (or 1 stick) chilled sweet butter, cut into 6 to 8 pieces
> 1 teaspoon salt
> 2–3 tablespoons ice water

Place all ingredients, except ice water, in food processor. Process until the mixture has the consistency of coarse meal. With the machine running, add water to the processor. Continue processing until mixture forms a ball. Refrigerate at least 30 minutes before using.

Yield: 1 nine-inch crust

Cuisinart processor: Steel knife blade

Other processors: Dough hook or other attachment manufacturer recommends for kneading

Pâte Brisée II

2 cups all-purpose flour
¼ pound (or 1 stick), plus 2 tablespoons chilled butter, cut into 8 pieces
1 teaspoon salt
1 egg
1½–2 tablespoons ice water

Place all ingredients, except water, in food processor. Process until the mixture has the consistency of coarse meal. With the machine running, add water to the processor. Continue processing until mixture forms a ball. Refrigerate at least 30 minutes before using.

Yield: 2 eight-inch crusts

Cuisinart processor: Steel knife blade

Other processors: Dough hook or other attachment manufacturer recommends for kneading

---

Pâte Brisée Sucrée I

1¾ cups all-purpose flour
Pinch of salt
2 tablespoons sugar
¼ pound plus 2 tablespoons sweet butter, chilled and cut into 8 pieces
2 tablespoonfuls vegetable shortening, chilled and cut into 2 pieces
3–4 tablespoons ice water

Place all ingredients, except water, in food processor. Process until the mixture has the consistency of coarse meal. With the machine running, add water to the processor. Continue processing until mixture forms a ball. Refrigerate at least 30 minutes before using.

Yield: 2 eight-inch crusts

Cuisinart processor: Steel knife blade

Other processors: Dough hook or other attachments manufacturer recommends for kneading

Pâte Brisée Sucrée II

1⅓ cups all-purpose flour
¼ pound sweet butter, chilled and cut into 6 or 8 pieces
Pinch of salt
1 tablespoon sugar
2–3 tablespoons ice water

Place all ingredients, except ice water, in food processor. Process until the mixture has the consistency of coarse meal. With the machine running, add water to the processor. Continue processing until mixture forms a ball. Refrigerate at least 30 minutes before using.

Yield: 1 nine-inch crust.

Cuisinart processor: Steel knife blade

Other processors: Dough hook or other attachments manufacturer recommends for kneading

Pâte Brisée Sucrée III

1¼ cups all-purpose flour
¼ pound chilled sweet butter, cut into 6 or 8 pieces
1 tablespoon sugar
¼ teaspoon salt
1 tablespoon ice water
1 egg

Place the first 4 ingredients in food processor and process until the mixture has the consistency of coarse meal. With the machine running, add the water and the egg and continue processing until mixture forms a ball.

Refrigerate at least 30 minutes before using.

Yield: 1 nine-inch crust

Cuisinart processor: Steel knife blade

Other processors: Dough hook or other attachment manufacturer recommends for kneading

All-American Pie Crust Dough

1 cup all-purpose flour
½ cup vegetable shortening
3–4 tablespoons ice water

Place flour and shortening in food processor and cut shortening into flour, turning the machine on and off, until mixture has consistency of coarse meal. Add ice water and continue processing until dough forms a ball.

Yield: 1 single 9-inch pie crust shell

Cuisinart processor: Steel knife blade

Other processors: Dough hook or other attachment manufacturer recommends for kneading

Mushroom and Onion Quiche

12 mushrooms
3 sprigs parsley
1 medium onion
3 tablespoons butter
3 eggs
1 cup light sweet cream
4 ounces imported Swiss cheese from Switzerland, cubed
½ teaspoon salt
¼ teaspoon white pepper
1 nine-inch unsweetened pâte brisée shell, partially baked*

Place mushrooms, parsley, and onion in food processor and chop. Heat butter in a skillet and sauté vegetables from processor until onions are lightly browned and mushrooms are cooked.

Place all remaining ingredients in processor, except *pâte brisée* shell, and process until thoroughly blended. Combine with mushroom-onion mixture and pour into partially baked, unsweetened *pâte brisée* shell. Place in preheated 375-degree oven for 35 to 40 minutes or until puffy and nicely browned. Knife inserted 1 inch from center should come out clean. Allow to cool for 10 minutes before serving.

* To partially bake *pâte brisée* shell: Roll out dough and fit into a 9-inch pie plate or quiche pan. Flute edges. Prick bottom of shell with a fork, and bake in a preheated 425-degree oven for 8 to 10 minutes. Cool before filling.

Serves: 6

Cuisinart processor: Steel knife blade

Other processors: Attachments manufacturer recommends for chopping and blending

Cheese and Onion Quiche

1 nine-inch unbaked pastry shell (see recipe, page 194, for Pâte Brisée I)
3 eggs, lightly beaten
4 ounces Swiss cheese, cut into cubes or strips
4 ounces Gruyère cheese, cut into cubes or strips
1 tablespoon flour
1 large onion
½ cup milk
½ cup light sweet cream
Salt and freshly ground white pepper to taste
¼ teaspoon nutmeg

Brush unbaked pastry shell with a little of the beaten eggs and chill.

Place cheeses in food processor and grate. Pour grated cheese into a bowl and stir in flour. Spoon cheese-flour combination into pastry shell.

Using food processor, slice onion thinly and place onion slices on top of grated cheese mixture in pastry shell.

Scald the milk and the cream, remove from heat, and add eggs, stirring for 30 seconds until blended. Season and pour over cheese and onion.

Bake in a preheated 425-degree oven for about 35 minutes or until knife inserted near the center comes out clean.

Serves: 6

Cuisinart processor: Shredding disc for cheeses; Slicing disc for onion

Other processors: Attachment manufacturer recommends for grating or shredding soft cheeses, and attachment for slicing onion

Crab Meat Quiche

1 nine-inch unbaked pastry shell (see recipe, page 194, for
   Pâte Brisée I)
4 eggs, lightly beaten
1 stalk celery, cut into 3 pieces
3 sprigs parsley
3 scallions, each cut into 3 pieces
1½ cups cooked crab meat, picked over and cartilage
   removed
2 tablespoons dry sherry wine
2 cups light sweet cream
Salt and freshly ground white pepper to taste
¼ teaspoon nutmeg

Brush unbaked pastry shell with a little of the beaten eggs and
chill.

Place celery, parsley, and scallions in food processor and chop
finely. Combine in a bowl with crab meat and sherry wine and
spoon vegetable-crab meat mixture into pastry shell.

Scald cream, remove from heat, and add eggs, stirring for 30
seconds until blended. Season and pour over vegetable-crab
meat mixture.

Bake in a preheated 425-degree oven for about 35 minutes or
until knife inserted near the center comes out clean.

Serves: 6

Cuisinart processor: Steel knife blade

Other processors: Attachment manufacturer recommends for
   chopping

Cannelloni

PASTA

2¼ cups all-purpose flour
3 eggs
¼ cup water
1 tablespoon oil

MEAT FILLING

¾ pound beef, trimmed and cut into cubes
¾ pound veal, trimmed and cut into cubes
1 chicken breast, boned, skinned, and cut into cubes
1 clove garlic
1 small onion
3 sprigs parsley
1 medium carrot, cut into 4 pieces
2 slices white bread, crusts trimmed, broken into large
    pieces
2 eggs

Place all ingredients for pasta in food processor and process,
turning machine on and off until dough forms a ball. Remove
from processor and refrigerate for at least 30 minutes.

While dough is refrigerating, place meat in food processor and
grind. You may have to do this in two or more steps. Grind
all remaining ingredients for meat filling and combine with
meat mixture until all ingredients are thoroughly combined.

Roll out dough on a well-floured board, as thinly as possible.
Cut dough into 4-inch squares. Cook squares (about 12 at a

time) in 6 quarts of rapidly boiling salted water for about 6 minutes. Dough squares should be *al dente*—slightly firm, not mushy. Remove dough squares from boiling water with a slotted spoon and drain, until all dough squares are cooked and drained.

Spoon about 3 tablespoons of filling onto each cooked square. Spread mixture on square, then roll the filled Canneloni square up and place seam side down in a large buttered baking dish. When all the Canneloni squares are in the baking dish, top evenly first with Mornay Sauce (page 74) and then with Italian Tomato Sauce (page 77).

Bake in preheated 350-degree oven for 25 minutes or until sauce is bubbling.

Serves: 6 to 8

Cuisinart processor: Steel knife blade

Other processors: Attachments manufacturer recommends for kneading or mixing dough, and for grinding

Gnocchi

1 pound medium potatoes, peeled, cut into cubes, boiled, and drained
2 tablespoons light sweet cream
2 tablespoons sweet butter
2 teaspoons chives
3 sprigs parsley
½ cup water
3 tablespoons butter
½ teaspoon salt
1 cup all-purpose flour

Place first five ingredients in food processor and blend until smooth.

Place water, 3 tablespoons butter, and salt in a saucepan and bring to a boil. Stir ½ cup of flour into water all at once, until mixture is combined. Heat mixture over medium-low heat for 2 to 3 minutes.

Put flour paste into food processor that contains potato mixture and process, turning machine on and off and scraping mixture down from sides of the bowl several times. Mixture will be sticky and heavy, therefore scraping down with the plastic spatula several times and turning machine on and off will help blend ingredients more quickly and put less of a strain on the motor.

Spoon mixture into a floured bowl and refrigerate for several hours.

Turn dough out onto a well-floured board and knead in remaining ½ cup of flour. At this point you should be able to work dough with your hands. If mixture still seems too sticky, add more flour, a little at a time.

Divide dough into 8 or 10 pieces. Roll each piece into a long strand that is about ½ inch thick. Cut each strand of dough into 2-inch lengths.

Poach gnocchi in boiling salted water for 2 to 3 minutes or until they rise to the top of the water.

Serve gnocchi in soup or with butter, heavy sweet cream, and grated Parmesan cheese to taste.

Serves: 6 to 8

Cuisinart processor: Steel knife blade

Other processors: Attachments manufacturer recommends for mixing, and a dough hook or other attachment recommended for kneading dough

JAMS, RELISHES, CHUTNEYS, AND NUT BUTTERS

Your food processor can turn a box of dried apricots into a beautiful smooth puree that's worthy of filling your finest crepes. It can chop ginger for chutney and fruits for relishes. It can chop nuts into the freshest nut butter you've ever tasted and produce cups of fresh bread crumbs from leftover loaves of French or Italian bread. Look over these recipes and discover how easily you can adapt your own favorite recipes to the food processor.

Apricot Jam

1 eleven–twelve-ounce box dried apricots
Water
1 cup sugar, or more, to taste

Place apricots in a large saucepan. Cover with water and cook over low heat until apricots are soft enough to be broken up with the back of a spoon. Allow apricots to cool in water and then pour into food processor and puree. You may have to do this in two or more steps. When all the apricots are thoroughly and smoothly pureed, return puree to saucepan, and over very, very low heat, start cooking the jam. Add sugar, half a cup at a time. Stir, and taste during cooking, and add more sugar if you wish.

Cook uncovered for approximately 1 hour or until jam is thick.

Test by putting a teaspoonful of jam on a plate and putting the plate in the refrigerator for 5 minutes. If the cooled puree is thick, you have apricot jam. Store covered in refrigerator or seal in sterilized jars.

This jam is especially delicious as a filling for rolled crepes.

Yield: Approximately 2 pints

Cuisinart processor: Steel knife blade

Other processors: Blender or attachment manufacturer recommends for pureeing

---

Georgia's Peachy Butter

4 pounds ripe peaches (about 20), peeled, halved, and pitted
2 cups sugar
1¼ teaspoons grated lemon rind
½ teaspoon cinnamon
¼ teaspoon cardamom

Place peaches in food processor and slice, using slicing disc. Remove to a large saucepan and cook in a small amount of water, stirring frequently, until peaches are soft. Return to food processor (now fitted with steel knife blade) and puree thoroughly.

Return peach puree to saucepan and combine with remaining ingredients. Cook over low heat until mixture thickens, about 45 minutes. Stir frequently.

Store, covered, in refrigerator, or seal in sterilized jars.

Yield: 2 pints

Cuisinart processor: Slicing disc for slicing peaches; Steel knife blade for pureeing peaches

Other processors: Use attachments manufacturer recommends for slicing and pureeing

Nectarine 'n' Tomato Jam, Country Style

1 pound fresh ripe nectarines (about 5 or 6), peeled, pitted, and halved
1 pound red ripe tomatoes, peeled and cored
¼ cup lemon juice
1 teaspoon grated lemon rind
¼ teaspoon ground allspice
1 one-and-three-quarter-ounce package powdered pectin
4 cups sugar

Place nectarines in food processor and chop. Remove to a large saucepan. Place tomatoes in food processor and chop. Add to nectarines.

Add lemon juice, lemon rind, allspice, and pectin and bring mixture to a hard boil. Stir in sugar and bring to a full, rolling boil. Boil hard for 1 minute.

Remove from heat and skim off foam. Seal in sterilized jars.

Yield: 5 eight-ounce jars

Cuisinart processor: Steel knife blade

Other processors: Attachment manufacturer recommends for chopping

NECTARINE 'N' TOMATO JAM
Courtesy California Tree Fruit Agreement

MINCEMEAT AND PEAR RELISH
Courtesy California Tree Fruit Agreement

Mincemeat and Pear Relish

2 cups prepared mincemeat
½ cup lemon juice
1½ teaspoons salt
1 teaspoon dry mustard
½ teaspoon rosemary
Dash of cayenne pepper
5 large Bartlett pears, cored and cut into quarters
1 small sweet red pepper, cored, seeded, and cut into 4 strips
1 small green pepper, cored, seeded, and cut into 4 strips

Combine mincemeat, lemon juice, salt, mustard, rosemary and cayenne in a large saucepan and heat mixture to boiling point over a medium heat.

Place pears in food processor. Chop pears and add to mincemeat mixture. Allow to simmer uncovered for 15 minutes. Chop 2 peppers in food processor and add to mincemeat-pear mixture. Cook for an additional 5 minutes. Store covered in refrigerator or seal in sterilized jars.

Yield: Approximately 1 quart

Cuisinart processor: Steel knife blade

Other processors: Attachment manufacturer recommends for fine chopping or dicing

Rajah's Special Chutney

4 ounces fresh ginger root, pared and cut into chunks
1½ cups water
Salt
3½ pounds fresh nectarines, halved and pitted
3½ cups sugar
1¼ cups vinegar
¼ cup Worcestershire sauce
2 cloves garlic
1 small onion
1 small canned green chili pepper
1 cup golden seedless raisins
½ cup fresh lime juice

Place ginger in food processor and chop or grate finely. Place ginger in a saucepan with water, add 2 tablespoons salt, and simmer about 20 minutes, or until ginger is almost tender.

Now using slicing disc, place nectarines in food processor, slice thinly, and reserve.

You may have to do this in two or more steps.

Drain ginger and reserve ¼ cup liquid. Mix this ginger liquid with sugar, 2 teaspoons salt, vinegar, and Worcestershire sauce. Place garlic and onion in food processor (now fitted with steel knife blade), chop, and add to ginger liquid mixture. Bring mixture to a boil.

Chop chili pepper in food processor and add to boiling mixture, along with nectarines, cooked ginger root, raisins, and lime juice, and cook over a low to medium heat until the mixture thickens. This will take about 1½ hours, and chutney will thicken even more as it chills. Seal in sterilized jars.

Yield: Approximately 8 half-pint jars

Cuisinart processor: Steel knife blade for chopping ginger, garlic, onion, and chili pepper; slicing disc for nectarines

Other processors: Attachments manufacturer recommends for chopping and slicing

Pecan Butter

2 cups pecans
2 tablespoons salad oil or butter
Salt to taste

Place pecans in food processor and process until pecans turn into a smooth paste. Pecans will form a ball. Process by turning machine on and off and scraping down mixture. Add oil or butter, continue processing, and add salt to taste.

Yield: 1 cup

Cuisinart processor: Steel knife blade

Other processors: Blender or attachment manufacturer recommends for making nut butters

Peanut Butter

To make peanut butter we recommend you use fresh-roasted peanuts in the shell. True, you do have to hand-shell them and remove the thin red skin that covers the nut, but the result—a creamy natural peanut butter—is well worth the trouble.

2 cups shelled and skinned roasted peanuts
Salt to taste

Place peanuts in food processor and process until the peanuts turn into a smooth paste. Process by turning machine on and off and scraping down the mixture from the sides of the bowl. Mixture will form a ball. Add salt to taste.

If peanut butter seems too stiff, continue processing until it softens.

Yield: 1 cup

Cuisinart processor: Steel knife blade

Other processors: Blender or attachment manufacturer recommends for making nut butters.

DESSERTS

For many people, dessert is the crowning event of the meal. Included in this chapter are recipes for such lavish desserts as Cream Puffs with Hot Fudge Sauce, Marble Strawberry Cheesecake, Southern Pecan Pie, Strawberry Tarts, Anise Cookies, and Chocolate Mousse—fitting finales to any meal. Impressive as these desserts may be, each is easy to prepare in the food processor. You may use these recipes as a guide to adapt your own dessert favorites for preparation in the food processor.

Cream Puffs with Hot Fudge Sauce

PUFF SHELLS (PÂTE À CHOUX)

1 cup water
4 tablespoons butter
1 teaspoon sugar
½ cup flour
2 eggs

CREAM FILLING

2 cups heavy sweet cream
1 tablespoon sugar
1 teaspoon vanilla

HOT FUDGE SAUCE

3 one-ounce squares semisweet chocolate
1 teaspoon vanilla
2–3 tablespoons sugar, to taste
¼ cup hot milk

To make puff shells, heat water and butter in a saucepan to boiling point. Using a wooden spoon, quickly stir in sugar and all the flour. Cook over low heat for about 2 minutes or until mixture coats the bottom of the pan and begins to move away from the sides. Cool slightly.

Place this *pâte à choux* in the food processor, add eggs one at a time, and process for several seconds or until the puff paste is shiny and smooth.

Drop puff paste by the tablespoonful onto a greased baking dish. Bake in a preheated 425-degree oven for 20 minutes. Lower temperature of oven to 375 degrees. Make a 1-inch slit in each puff and continue baking for approximately 10 minutes longer or until puffs are nicely browned and crusty. Remove from oven and cool. Cut tops off puffs and scoop out uncooked portion from within each puff.

Place cream in food processor and start whipping, gradually adding sugar and vanilla, until thickened. Watch carefully and do not overprocess, or the result will be butter.

Fill cooled puffs with cream and cover with tops of puffs. Refrigerate.

Place all ingredients for sauce in food processor and process until sauce is well blended. Spoon sauce over puffs and serve.

Serves: 8

Cuisinart processor: Steel knife blade

Other processors: Attachments manufacturer recommends for kneading and mixing dough, for whipping cream, and for grating and blending sauce

Chocolate Mousse

1 six-ounce package semisweet chocolate pieces
¼ cup, or 5 tablespoons, hot, black, strong coffee
2 tablespoons sugar
4 egg yolks
2 tablespoons dark rum
4 eggs whites, stiffly beaten

Place chocolate pieces in food processor and chop finely, turning machine on and off and scraping chocolate down from sides of the bowl. Add hot coffee and sugar and process until blended.

Add egg yolks and rum gradually and continue processing until mixture is well blended. Pour mixture into a bowl and fold in egg whites. Chill thoroughly before serving.

Serves: 8

Cuisinart processor: Steel knife blade

Other processors: Blender or attachments manufacturer recommends for fine chopping or grating, and for beating or whipping

Aunt Clara's Chocolate Chip Cake

¼ **pound sweet butter, cut into 6 or 8 pieces**
1 **cup sugar**
2 **eggs**
½ **cup milk**
½ **teaspoon vanilla extract**
1¾ **cups all-purpose flour**
½ **teaspoon salt**
2 **teaspoons baking powder**
½ **cup semisweet chocolate bits**

Place butter, sugar, eggs, milk, and vanilla in food processor. Process until ingredients are blended. Add flour, salt, and baking powder gradually to food processor. Turn the machine on and off while processing and process only as long as it takes flour to disappear into other ingredients. Pour into a buttered 9-inch cake pan and stir in chocolate bits.

Bake for 25 minutes in a preheated 375-degree oven. Allow to cool, and cut into squares before serving.

Serves: 6 to 8

Cuisinart processor: Steel knife blade

Other processors: Attachment manufacturer recommends for mixing

Creamy Pear Ice

3 large Bartlett pears
½ cup pineapple juice
1 cup sugar
½ teaspoon salt
1 three-ounce package cream cheese, cut into 3 pieces
½ cup heavy sweet cream
2 tablespoons lemon juice

Peel, core, and cut each pear into 4 pieces. Place pears and pineapple juice in food processor and process until a smooth puree is attained. Add sugar, salt, cream cheese, sweet cream, and lemon juice gradually to processor and continue processing until well blended. Pour into a loaf pan or other container, cover, and freeze overnight.

Several hours before serving, cut Pear Ice into chunks and place in food processor. Blend quickly until smooth, spoon into container, cover, and return to freezer. Freeze again before serving.

Serves: 6 to 8

Cuisinart processor: Steel knife blade

Other processors: Blender or attachment manufacturer recommends for mixing

CREAMY PEAR ICE
Courtesy California Tree Fruit Agreement

Spicy Lettuce Bars
with Lemon Frosting

¼ head iceberg lettuce, cut into pieces
1½ cups all-purpose flour
2 teaspoons baking powder
½ teaspoon baking soda
½ teaspoon salt
⅛ teaspoon ground mace
⅛ teaspoon ground ginger
1 cup sugar
½ cup salad oil
1½ teaspoons grated lemon rind
2 eggs
½ cup walnuts

Place lettuce in food processor and chop. Sift flour with baking powder, baking soda, salt, and spices. Add to processor and combine. Gradually add sugar, oil, and lemon rind to processor and combine. Add eggs one at a time and continue processing. Add walnuts and process mixture until well blended and walnuts are coarsely chopped.

Spoon batter into a greased 9×13-inch pan. Bake in a preheated 350-degree oven for 30 minutes. Cool, cut into bars, and frost with Lemon Frosting.

Yield:　12 to 15 bars

Cuisinart processor:　Steel knife blade

Other processors:　Attachment manufacturer recommends for mixing

LEMON FROSTING

1½ cups confectioner's sugar
¼ teaspoon lemon extract
½ teaspoon grated lemon rind
3 tablespoons milk
1 tablespoon sweet butter

Place all ingredients in food processor and blend until mixture is thoroughly smooth. Spread on Spicy Lettuce Bars.

Cuisinart processor: Steel knife blade

Other processors: Blender or attachment manufacturer recommends for mixing

❧❧❧

Strawberry Tarts with Crème Pâtissière

TART SHELLS

> 1¼ cups all-purpose flour
> ¼ pound chilled sweet butter, cut into 6 or 8 pieces
> 1 tablespoon sugar
> ¼ teaspoon salt
> 1 tablespoon cold water
> 1 egg

Place the first 4 ingredients in food processor and process until the mixture has the consistency of coarse meal. With the machine running, add the water and the egg and continue processing until mixture forms a ball. Refrigerate at least 30 minutes before using.

Roll out dough and press into individual small tart pans. Prick each shell with a fork at bottom and sides. Trim edges, and flute with your fingers. Place tart shells on a baking sheet and bake in a preheated 400-degree oven for about 10 to 15 minutes or until shells are delicately brown. Cool before filling.

Yield: 6 small tart shells

Cuisinart processor: Steel knife blade

Other processors: Dough hook or other attachment manufacturer recommends for kneading

CRÈME PÂTISSIÈRE

⅓ cup sugar
3½ tablespoons cornstarch
6 lightly beaten egg yolks
2 cups milk
½ tablespoon vanilla extract
2 tablespoons Grand Marnier liqueur

Combine sugar, cornstarch, and egg yolks in a saucepan. Scald the milk and pour it gradually over egg mixture. Cook over low heat, stirring constantly with a wire whisk or egg beater until mixture is thick and smooth. Keep heat low and do not allow the mixture to come to a boil. After removing from heat, stir in vanilla and Grand Marnier. Cool before filling tart shells.

Yield: About 3 cups

Assembling Tarts:

6 tart shells
1 cup red currant glaze, prepared by cooking 1 cup of red
   currant jelly with two tablespoonfuls of sugar, until thick
Crème Pâtissière
1 pint fresh strawberries, washed and hulled

Paint inside of each tart shell with currant glaze and allow to cool for about 5 minutes. Fill each tart shell about two thirds full with *crème pâtissière*. Arrange fresh strawberries close together around edge of each tart and in center, with points up. Spoon more currant glaze over strawberries and refrigerate tarts until you're ready to serve them.

Serves: 6

Cheesecakes

Food processors seem to have been designed for the creation of delicate, light cheesecakes. Practically everyone has a favorite cheesecake, and while we can't include recipes for all the variations, we have selected a representative sample ranging from strawberry, chocolate, and cherry cheesecake to ricotta cheesecake and a Hungarian favorite, pot cheese and fresh dill cheesecake.

Cherry Cheese Pie in Graham Cracker Crumb Crust

CRUST

12 graham crackers, broken into large pieces
1 tablespoon sugar
¼ cup butter, melted

FILLING

2 eight-ounce packages cream cheese, each cut into 4 pieces
¾ cup sugar
4 eggs
1 cup sour cream
1 tablespoon all-purpose flour
1 teaspoon vanilla
2 teaspoons lemon juice
¼ cup half-and-half
1 one-pound-five-ounce can cherry pie filling

To make crust, place graham cracker pieces in food processor and process until you have fine crumbs. Add sugar and continue processing until well mixed. Pour crumb-sugar mixture into a bowl and add butter, mixing until crumbs are moistened. Press crumbs into a 9- or 10-inch buttered pie plate and chill before using.

For filling, place cream cheese and sugar in food processor and blend until creamy. Add all remaining ingredients, except cherry pie filling, and continue processing until smooth.

Pour cheese mixture into pie shell and bake in a preheated 350-degree oven for 45 to 55 minutes or until a toothpick inserted an inch from the center comes out dry.

Turn oven off and allow pie to cool in oven for 15 to 20 minutes. Top of cheesecake may crack during baking. This will not affect the flavor in any way.

Refrigerate for at least 4 hours and then top with cherry pie filling.

Serves: 8

Cuisinart processor: Steel knife blade

Other processors: Blender or attachments manufacturer recommends for grinding and for mixing

CHERRY CHEESE PIE IN GRAHAM CRACKER CRUMB CRUST
Courtesy of United Dairy Industry Association

Marble Strawberry Cheesecake

1 nine-inch unbaked French pastry shell made with sugar (Pâte Brisée Sucrée II; see page 196)

3 eight-ounce packages cream cheese, softened, each package cut into 4 pieces

1 cup sugar

3 eggs

1 cup sour cream

2 tablespoons all-purpose flour

1 six-ounce package semisweet chocolate pieces, melted

1 cup whipped cream

2 twelve-ounce packages frozen strawberries, thawed and drained

Line the bottom and sides of a 9-inch springform pan with Pâte Brisée Sucrée II. Prick dough at the bottom and place in a preheated 425-degree oven for about 10 minutes or until lightly browned. Set aside and allow to cool.

Place the next 5 ingredients in the food processor and process until completely smooth and blended. Pour melted chocolate into food processor and turn machine on and off *immediately*. Overprocessing will result in a chocolate cheesecake rather than a marble cheesecake.

Pour marbled mixture into cooled pastry shell. Bake in a preheated 350-degree oven for about 1 hour. Turn oven off and allow cheesecake to remain in oven for an additional hour. Refrigerate for at least 6 hours before serving.

Before serving, remove sides from pan. Spread whipped cream over top of cake. Spoon strawberries on top.

Serves: 8

Cuisinart processor: Steel knife blade

Other processors: Blender or attachment manufacturer recommends for mixing

Italian Ricotta Cheese Pie

PASTRY SHELL

2 cups all-purpose flour
⅛ teaspoon salt
½ cup sugar
¼ cup butter, cut into 4 pieces
3 egg yolks, beaten
1 tablespoon milk
4 tablespoons water

FILLING

1½ pounds ricotta cheese
1½ cups sugar
4 eggs
1 teaspoon vanilla extract
2 teaspoons lemon juice
Grated rind of ½ lemon
½ cup semisweet chocolate pieces
½ cup glazed citron

Place all ingredients for pastry crust, except milk and water, in food processor. Process until the mixture has the consistency of coarse meal. With the machine running, add milk and water, gradually, until mixture forms a ball. Remove dough. Refrigerate dough for 3 to 4 hours.

Place all ingredients for filling, except chocolate and citron, in food processor and blend until smooth.

Divide dough in half. Roll out ½ dough and fit into the bottom of a 9- or 10-inch pie plate, making sure to have a 1-inch overhang of dough around the edge of the pie plate.

Fill crust with ricotta mixture and stir in chocolate pieces and citron.

Roll out remainder of dough for a lattice top. To make lattice, cut narrow strips of pastry and weave them, forming the latticework, on floured board or piece of waxed paper. Slip lattice on top of the pie.

Trim and seal edges by folding bottom crust over top. Flute edges. Bake in a preheated 350-degree oven for 50 to 60 minutes or until top is puffed and golden brown.

Serves: 8

Cuisinart processor: Steel knife blade

Other processors: Attachments manufacturer recommends for kneading dough, and for mixing or blending

Hungarian Dilly Cheesecake

CRUST

1¼ cups flour
½ pound sweet butter, cut into 10 to 12 pieces
2 egg yolks
⅓ cup sugar
½ teaspoon baking powder
Grated rind of ½ lemon
Pinch of salt
2 tablespoons sour cream

FILLING

2 eggs, separated
½ pound pot cheese
½ cup sugar
¼ teaspoon vanilla extract
1 tablespoon lemon juice
4 tablespoons minced fresh dill
1 egg beaten with 1 tablespoon milk

Place flour and butter in food processor and process until mixture has the consistency of coarse crumbs. Add egg yolks, sugar, baking powder, lemon rind, salt, and sour cream. Process until mixture is blended. Remove dough and refrigerate for 30 minutes.

Take chilled dough and roll out three quarters of it in a 9-inch square baking pan. Prick dough with a fork at the bottom and bake in a preheated 375-degree oven for 10 minutes.

To make filling:
Place egg whites in processor and beat until stiff. Reserve.

Place cheese, egg yolks, sugar, vanilla, and lemon juice in food processor and blend. Remove to bowl, fold in egg whites, and stir in dill.

Spread cheese filling on partially baked dough.

Roll out remainder of the dough for a lattice top. To make lattice, cut narrow strips of pastry and weave them, forming the latticework, on a floured board or piece of waxed paper. Slip lattice on top of cheesecake.

Brush latticework strips with egg-milk mixture. Place cake in a preheated 375-degree oven and bake for an additional half hour.

Allow cake to cool, and cut into squares before serving.

Serves: 6 to 8

Cuisinart processor: Steel knife blade

Other processors: Attachments manufacturer recommends for kneading dough, beating, and for mixing

Southern Pecan Pie

1 eight-inch unbaked All-American Pie Crust (see page 198)
½ cup sugar
2 tablespoons butter
2 eggs
2 tablespoons flour
¼ teaspoon salt
1 teaspoon almond extract
1 teaspoon vanilla extract
1 cup light corn syrup
2 cups pecans

Prepare pie crust dough, fit into an 8-inch pie plate, and set aside.

Place all filling ingredients, except pecans, in food processor and blend thoroughly. Add 1½ cups pecans and process briefly, until pecans are coarsely chopped.

Pour filling into pie crust and sprinkle remaining pecans on top. Bake in a preheated 350-degree oven for 30 to 45 minutes or until filling is set.

Serves: 6

Cuisinart processor: Steel knife blade

Other processors: Attachments manufacturer recommends for mixing or blending, and grinding

---

ESPRESSO BLACK BOTTOM PIE
Courtesy Medaglia d'Oro Espresso Coffee

Espresso Black Bottom Pie

CRUST

18 zwieback biscuits, broken into large pieces
2 tablespoons sugar
⅓ cup melted butter

FILLING

2 tablespoons cornstarch
¼ cup sugar
¼ teaspoon salt
2 cups brewed espresso coffee
4 egg yolks
2 one-ounce squares semisweet chocolate, melted
1 envelope gelatin
1 teaspoon vanilla extract
4 egg whites
½ cup sugar
1 cup heavy sweet cream
2 tablespoons sugar

To make crust, place zwieback pieces in food processor and process until you have fine crumbs. Add sugar and continue processing until well mixed. Pour crumb-sugar mixture into a bowl and add butter, mixing until crumbs are moistened. Press mixture firmly into bottom and sides of an ungreased 9-inch pie plate and chill.

In a 1-quart saucepan, mix cornstarch, sugar, and salt. Stir in coffee and egg yolks. Stir constantly over low heat until sauce bubbles and thickens. Remove from heat; pour 1 cup of the sauce into a small bowl and stir in melted chocolate.

In a cup, mix gelatin and ¼ cup water. Stir gelatin mixture into remaining hot coffee sauce. Stir in vanilla.

Cool chocolate and coffee mixtures separately.

Spread cool chocolate mixture evenly into bottom of crumb-lined pie plate.

Place egg whites in food processor and beat until they thicken. Gradually add sugar until mixture is stiff and glossy.

Fold egg whites into coffee mixture, which will have thickened as it cools, and then spread coffee mixture over chocolate mixture in pie plate.

Place heavy cream in food processor and whip, adding sugar gradually, until cream is thick. Garnish pie with cream.

Serves: 6 to 8

Cuisinart processor: Steel knife blade

Other processors: Attachments manufacturer recommends for grinding, and beating or whipping

French Apple Pie

6 large tart apples, peeled, cored, and cut into quarters
¼ cup raisins
¾ cup brown sugar
1 tablespoon flour
1 tablespoon lemon juice
1 teaspoon cinnamon
¼ teaspoon nutmeg
1 tablespoon butter
2 nine-inch pâte brisée sucrée crusts, unbaked

Slice apples in food processor and remove to bowl. Add raisins, brown sugar, flour, lemon juice, cinnamon, and nutmeg to apples and stir thoroughly.

Spoon apple mixture into prepared pie shell. Dot with butter. Cover filling with top crust. Press to seal, and flute edges. Prick top generously with a fork. Bake in a pre-heated 400-degree oven for 35 minutes or until brown.

Serves: 8

Cuisinart processor: Slicing disc

Other processors: Attachment manufacturer recommends for slicing

Crepes Filled with Jam

1 cup all-purpose flour
¼ cup sugar
3 eggs
2 tablespoons melted butter
1½ cups milk
⅛ teaspoon salt
2 teaspoons grated lemon rind
½ pound (or 2 sticks) sweet butter
8 ounces of jam

Place flour, sugar, eggs, and butter in food processor. Start machine and add the milk gradually. Add salt and lemon rind and continue processing until batter has the consistency of light cream. Pour crepe batter into a bowl or pitcher and let it rest in the refrigerator for 2 hours before using.

To cook crepes:

Lightly butter one or two 6-inch teflon-coated skillets. Using a small ladle, spoon enough batter into pan to coat bottom. Tilt pan so crepe batter spreads evenly. Cook until lightly browned and then slide out of pan onto a flat plate. Allow crepe to cool, then fill with your favorite jam (homemade apricot is best), and roll.

Place rolled crepes in a baking dish and heat for 15 minutes in a preheated 350-degree oven before serving. Crepes may be made the day before, and as you become adept at crepe making, you'll be able to use two crepe pans without any trouble.

Serves: 8 (2 crepes apiece)

Cuisinart processor: Steel knife blade

Other processors: Blender or attachment manufacturer recommends for mixing

Sugar Cookies

¼ **pound sweet butter, cut into 6 or 8 pieces**
1 cup sugar
1 egg
1 tablespoon light sweet cream
½ **teaspoon vanilla extract**
½ **teaspoon salt**
1 teaspoon baking powder
1½ **cups all-purpose flour**

Place butter and sugar in food processor and process until combined. Add egg, cream, and vanilla and process until blended. Gradually add salt, baking powder, and flour to food processor and process until blended.

Drop tablespoonfuls of cookie mixture onto a buttered baking sheet. Bake in a preheated 375-degree oven for about 8 minutes.

Yield: About 2 dozen cookies

Cuisinart processor: Steel knife blade

Other processors: Attachment manufacturer recommends for mixing

SUGAR COOKIE VARIATIONS

Walnut Cookies: Add ⅓ cup finely chopped walnuts

Coconut Cookies: Add ½ cup finely chopped coconut

Lemon Cookies: Add ½ teaspoons lemon extract, plus 2 teaspoons grated lemon rind, and omit vanilla

Maple Cookies: Use crushed maple sugar in place of white sugar

Christmas Cookies: Sprinkle with colored sugar while cookies are still hot

Raisin Cookies: Add ½ cup chopped raisins

❀❀*❀*

Anise Cookies

¾ **cup sugar**
¼ **cup butter**
¼ **cup sour cream**
1 **egg**
1 **teaspoon vanilla extract**
1 **teaspoon anise extract**
1¼ **cups flour**
½ **teaspoon baking soda**
¼ **teaspoon salt**

Place sugar and butter in food processor and process until combined. Add sour cream, egg, vanilla, and anise. Process until blended. Combine flour, baking soda, and salt and add to food processor gradually, ½ cup at a time. Process until blended.

Drop tablespoonfuls of cookie mixture onto a buttered baking sheet. Bake in a preheated 350-degree oven for 10 to 12 minutes.

Yield: About 2 dozen cookies

Cuisinart processor: Steel knife blade

Other processors: Attachment manufacturer recommends for mixing

INDEX

Spicy lettuce bars with lemon
    frosting, 224
Spinach puree, creamy, 167
Spring salad dip, 41
Steak tartare, 108
    and caviar, 109
Strawberry tarts with crème
    pâtissière, 227
Swedish meatballs, 102
Swedish tea ring, 188
Sweet potato pudding, 164

Tacos, Texas, 110
Taramasalata, 35
Tartar sauce, 68
Texas tacos, 110
Three-bean fiesta salad, 152
Tomato(es):
    baked, for Gallatin's spiced
        stuffed, 157
    -nectarine jam, 210
    sauce, 76
        Italian, 77
    spiced stuffed, Gallatin's, 156
T. T. Wang's green pepper puffs,
    30
T. T. Wang's shrimp strawberries,
    29

Tuna:
    -avocado spread, 36
    butter, 44
    -shrimp pie, 138
    timbale, 140
    vitello tonnato, 94
Turkey:
    burgers with fruit glaze, 116
    mousse San Francisco, 114
    -pear chili, 118

Veal:
    -chicken pâté *en croûte*, 86
    vitello tonnato, 94
Vichyssoise, 53
Vitello tonnato, 94

Walnut sauce, sweet, for egg
    noodles, 69
Whole wheat braid bread, 190
White bean and chestnut puree,
    165

Zucchini:
    lamb-stuffed, 113
    in sour cream and dill sauce,
        170